My Poems

Oskar Klausenstock, M.D.

MY POEMS

iUniverse books may be ordered through booksellers or by contacting:

iUniverse
1663 Liberty Drive
Bloomington, IN 47403
www.iuniverse.com
1-800-Authors (1-800-288-4677)

ISBN: 978-1-4917-4149-8 (sc)
ISBN: 978-1-4917-4148-1 (e)

Library of Congress Control Number: 2014912638

Printed in the United States of America.

iUniverse rev. date: 07/15/2014

By way of commitment to the arts, allow me to dedicate these lines to all my kin with all my love and affection

Contents

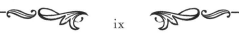

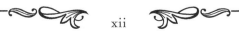

To Notice

I noticed the wind
By the flutter of aspen leaves,
The biting cold
By the flushed cheeks of a smiling child.

I noticed the rain
In the splashing of a passing car,
The tortoise shells of umbrellas,
The quick-stepping passerby.

I noticed the passing of time
By the tremor of my hand,
The many lines across my brow,
The missing leaves from my calendar.

I noticed the pain
In the near emptiness
Of my medicine vial,
The puffy eyelids of unsleeping nights.

The Wanderer

By some capricious genesis
I've become a snowflake,
Swirling afloat, windblown,
Beating my crystal wings.

The butterfly of winter—
I search, I seek to find
A perch within the spirals
Of a winter's gale
To stay suspended
Amid the heavens in my travail.

Created by the whim
Of northern currents,
Wintry gales, some distant shore,
And ever-changing tides of air,
I flutter, heedlessly I soar.

I live and yet I know
That soon I too shall fall
And down on earth
Commingle with my sister flakes
To be the mantle of white snow.

But not yet shall I die.
First I shall add
A sparkle to the frosty earth,
To all the crystals,
The wintry canopy of life.

And when the sun shall rise,
Our summon to return
From where we came,
I and my sister flakes
Will readily obey.

Although trodden down,
I shall rise once again,
And like a crystal phoenix
Of snowy ashes born
To soar, to soar, to soar.

To Atone

Give me back my wings so I can fly
Across the span of time
And look upon the years gone by.

So I can fly once more
And in my retrospective flight
Undo the harm I've done.

So I can soar
And, with a newfound wing,
Heal wounds inflicted by the war.

And in that flight
Gaze at the hurt, the pain,
The sorrow-laden sight.

Let me undo the many slights,
Wing-beat my breast in penance
Before it is too late to fly.

On Writing Poems

There are days when words
Well shaped, as on parade,
Law-abiding, amenable of sorts,
Stand arms and legs in perfect rhyme.

There are fallow, rainy days,
Each word a silent man with shuffling feet,
Bent forward with his hidden face
Beneath the canopy of his umbrella.

Words frosty, chilling, the skies dark,
Lame men standing in line,
Waiting before a closed door of the mind,
Waiting and not knowing why.

Then comes the day of sunlit words,
Light, brisk, a child hopping on one leg,
A soaring butterfly capricious in its flight,
A jingle full of rhythm and rhyme.

And I, the juggler and the mime,
Stand mute, my eyes half-closed, and then
My words walk by, tiptoeing slowly or in haste,
And I stand there to offer them my pen.

Of Times Gone By

I knew a time when words were paltry,
Harsh, travesties of their intent.
Love and godliness were hate misspelled
To deceive others, to deceive oneself.

Of songs forgotten and human voices
Reduced to shouts or pity-laden whimpers,
When language was the tool to whip,
To fan the gnawing pain of fear.

The sun, concealed by hate, had ceased to shine,
Another ice age settled on the land,
And words, once warm, invented to caress,
Froze on each speaker's lips.

When songs became a drumbeat,
Hollow sound of hobnailed boots,
The roar of warplanes carried by the wind,
The rattling of a jailer's chain.

Muted now those sounds, only a vague echo
Of punctured drums remain.
Ancient words, once toppled from their pedestal,
Rose from the dust and found their stance again.

Only so many mothers wordlessly still weep,
One for her little child,
An aging father for his only son.

Noah and the Deluge

Look out there, Noah,
See what God has wrought
To try his genesis anew.
Capriciously he drowned all men,
Sparing only animals and you.

Stay hidden, Noah, in your hand-hewn ark;
The time to leave is not at hand.
The only bird on Ararat, a raven bird of doom,
It is a dove in camouflage, all white and bland.

Beware, the bird of your delusion
Is merely a bird of prey,
The olive branch, a deadly hemlock bough,
Not the proverbial gift of peace.

Its flight is not the tiding of goodwill;
It is a flight of terror
At what your God has done,
His caw, a stifled sob, a cry.

It's winter, Noah,
The earth still desolate, forlorn.
The birds of peace are still to come.
The spring is far away.

Alone on Ararat, your gift of speech
No animal could fathom.
God drowned all men.
To be forever silent is your bane.

Look out there, Noah, take another drink.
Look at the giant rainbow far away.
It's not a covenant, old man.
It's only one more gate to hell.

A Poem to Be Clever

Dear Dr. McDrever,
Don't utter the word *never*,
For life, unpredictable,
Is without rules whatever.

And your priest, Father McTever,
With prayers of a kingdom forever,
Be more contrite,
For men will sin again and whenever.

Come, don't you weep, dear Miss Plever,
The dumb among us and the clever,
Even the strongest rope that binds
Some man will eventually sever.

So let us cheer today or whenever,
For life has no rules whatsoever.
The sun will rise, the sun will set,
Whether we live only a day or forever.

Myths

I was a swirling electron
Seduced by the center of an atom.
Before I knew, I was a molecule
In an infinity of matter.

A strange contraption caught my eye,
Double and helical, twisted on itself,
Slender and alluring,
I fell under its spell.

The ecstasy of being
Surged through my testicular domain,
Concealed in her cortical ovarian abode,
I was seduced by a rosy-cheeked maiden.

Insatiably hungry by a need to be,
By an inexplicable cosmic appetite,
Defiant, unrepentant, I shall become a she,
Or if I wish I might become a he,
The poet of illusory existence.

The Historical Apple Tree

Lulled by the shade of verdant branches
Of my alluring apple tree,
I rest against the verdant trunk,
Gaze at my sun-bracing friends
With awe and love, half-drunk,
And speak to them in apple idiom words.

I see you there, old friend of mine, red-cheeked,
You temptress apple, the serpent's swain,
Alluring, beckoning with wily reptile words.
You were the cause for men to toil
And women to bear men in labor pain.

And you there, clutching with your stem
The drooping, tired branch,
The apple Paris gave to Aphrodite
In Hella's contest of the Gods,
The cause of strife, the cause of blight.

And over there, concealed by leaves,
You impudent and brazen thing
That woke old Newton from his sleep
To let him know why man must walk
And birds must fly on a wing.

Hide not beneath the drooping branch.
Look at the sun with pride,
The William Tells of apple tale,
Guiding his arrow
To see his child free from assail.

And you, the bashful,
Sun-kissed fruit beneath that other branch,
A loving mother's apple of her eye,
The way she gazes at her babe,
Suckling at her breast to still its cry.

Fat, luscious apple near the pinnacle above,
Don't brag so much, don't glow
By being the quintessence of America,
The content of cold cider,
Of motherhood and pie.

And you up there, so proud,
You apple of invention,
Playmate of Macintosh and Macs,
Of dot-coms and of rams,
Minus a byte from your dimension.
And you, the shameless apple,
To be partaken once a day,
A doctor's bane, the illness's foe,
The guardian of man's health,
Another covenant man must obey.

And all the rest of you with crimson cheeks,
And you, the paler ones within the canopy of leaves,
The wormy, pockmarked, pincushions for a hungry beak,
Soon I shall pluck you too,
My dreamer's apples on my tree.

Confessions

I ain't no poet, no rhymer, and no bard,
Only a doodler of random words
On the margins of my daily life.

Ain't got no magic
In my threadbare sleeves,
No stovepipe hat,
No tricks, no subterfuge.

I'm only a pickpocket
On the loose,
A restless vagrant,
Stealing a word here and there.

A panhandler squatting
On the sidewalk grate,
Hand outstretched, palm up,
Begging for a thought.

But on a sandy shore,
A full moon, a starlit night,
Alone and swaddled
In the blanket of my past.

Unbidden and unasked-for
Words come at last,
Life-giving, zestful,
Rushing at me with the tide.

Of Sounds

Dawn enters through the murky autumn panes,
A naked maple branch sun-kissed aglow,
My wake-up call, the end of dreams,
In slow and gentle tremolo.

The days are short, the nights too long,
The tardy eastern sky, a thespian on the stage
Reluctant to commence to read his lines
In hesitant ritardando.

The summits of the trees light up,
Ablaze like Sabbath candles,
Aflame and eager for the morning sun,
In sprightly scherzo.

Down in the street and wide awake,
The milkman's wheels
Rattle on the cobbled pavement stones
In ragtime beat accelerando.

The church bells rend the silence,
The old familiar matinee,
Loud and overwhelming
In shrill vibrato.

The drumbeat on the wooden stairs,
The schoolboy's footsteps,
Late for school again,
In swift staccato.

My sloe-eyed next-door neighbor sings,
Soft voiced, the same refrain,
Rehearsing for the night
In soft bel canto.

The day drifts by, simple and mundane.
My hands upon the keyboard
Speed up and then slow again
In largo or andante chord.

Night calls upon my nodding head,
My weary, tired eye.
The pillow sings my lullaby,
A nocturne for the hunter in the sky.

Circus

Come, enter my enticing circus tent
Of flimflam, fallacy, and delusions.
Look at the fat lady prancing on the stage,
Her bulging cheeks, her hair brick red,
While in the alleyway a hungry child
Begs for a crumb of bread.

Look, the clown is standing on his head,
Tears running from his painted eyes,
His twitching bulbous nose,
His baggy pants, his floppy shoes.
Look, clap your hands and smile,
While out there thousands weep.

Look at the doggy on its hind legs,
A blue ball balanced on its muzzle,
And doves of peace aflutter at the apex of the tent,
A China man suspended by his plait,
While in the town square in neat rows
Stand men with hobnailed boots and wait.

Dance

Dance with me,
My arms still strong,
While hand in hand we touch,
Our feet in duet song.

Dance with me,
Become my rhythm, become my rhyme,
In ever-faster glide,
A dervish trance, a dance sublime.

And dancing let us be
The tumbling mountain brook
Before we turn
Into the calm and placid sea.

Before the winter comes
To claim the lustfulness
Of youthful limbs
And gold turns into silver crowns.

Our frowns, our smiles become deep etched
Upon our brow,
Our eyes unclouded yet,
Our ears attuned to whispers in the night.

Let us dance with grace
While days are longer than a wintry night
And our breaths remain
A pleasure's sigh.

The Wedding of Mary McCloy

Smile now, my dear Mary McCloy,
The sweetest lass of Dundee,
This a day full of joy,
A day full of glee,
Red roses, red cheeks, eyes aglow.

Come, blushing bride
And you pomaded groom,
The wedding guests are in their pew,
The preacher's fingering the ring,
Yer life's about to start anew.

The preacher spoke,
Yer knees still sore,
But the ring's on yer finger.
Ye've kissed and embraced,
The man ye adore.

The banns have been read.
Ye both tied the knot,
One flesh now, one wedded pair.
The bells are still ringing.
Rice floats in the air.

The bridesmaids are envious.
The groom beams with pride.
Yer papa is grinnin', yer mama in tears,
Yer sisters and brothers,
Well-wishers and cheers.

The time to dance is now at hand,
So stomp yer feet and twist yer rear.
The piper is piping his tune,
The banjo's strumming,
The sun is bright, it's nearly high noon.

No need to be sad,
Each lad has a lassie,
And for each lassie a lad.
So let us loudly clap our hands.
Today let's be merry and forever be glad.

Sleep, My Child

Sleep, my child,
Rest against my breast.
The sandman's at the gate.
Your eyes are heavy.
The hour is late.

Sleep, dream, your prince resides
In his palace on the hill,
The marble floor,
A thousand candles lit,
The music plays.

Sleep, do not gaze
Upon the earthen floor,
Adobe walls, the barren shelves,
The howling of the hungry wolves.
Let not the biting wind
Become your cradlesong.

Dream on, my child,
For all your dreams
Someday will come to naught.
Princes, palaces are a disguise,
And all the fairy tales
Of lands of milk and honey
Are only man-made lies.

Embers

Let me sit at the open hearth,
Hands outstretched, eyes gazing
At the embers of today,
And remember
The glow of days gone by.

Their gentle radiance on the wane,
Wrapped in an ashen skin,
The light a little dim,
The glow, the scent,
The zest to live to dream,
As yet not wholly spent.

Each ember, a sepia page of yesterday,
Pressed flowers, autumn leaves
Upon the unread pages yet to turn.
To be caressed by trembling hands,
A windswept hum,
A song, merely a refrain.

Sleep now, do not awake the crackling flames,
The sleeping dogs of war,
The stench of burning flesh,
Birth mothers of so many embers of the past,
At times to be recalled afresh.

A gust of wind—ill-wanted guest of time—
The sleeping embers come to life
And glow anew of days gone by,
Of days concealed, days stashed away.
I beg of you,
Just let me watch the embers of today.

The Grain of Sand

The sandman shook the sieve,
A grain of sand, I drifted,
One among the millions,
Without reason, without rhyme.

One by one fell by the way,
Though clinging to the grate of life,
And when the night became a day,
Only I was left to stay.

Why me? Why me, Mr. Sandman,
Without heart and without guile?
Asked I, the only left.
The Sandman grinned his crooked smile.
"Befehl," he said. "I must obey."

"Unwanted men must die,"
The Sandman said. "It's our way."
No rhyme, and without reason,
He spoke without a tear and went away.

The Pilgrimage to Majdanek

Into a barren land he cast his seeds,
And misbegotten
Each grew into nettle weeds.
The rose he kissed at dawn
Wilted at dusk.
The woman he loved yesterday
All too soon forgot his name.

Long was the trek for the man from Ur
To pitch his tent in a foreign land.
Tired and spent, he wished it to be home.
Gazing at the doves of peace with tired eyes,
He failed to see the falcons overhead.

White is his beard, baggy his eyelids,
Stooped is the back of the man from Ur.
He searched for a stone
To place beneath his head,
But all were bespoken,
Each at the head of a mound of earth.

Softly wept the man from Ur,
Dry-eyed, he wept,
For in that long and arduous trek
Through deserts, parting seas, and arid plains,
The sands of exile drank his tears,
The vultures feasted on his heart.

And so he sat on the mound of earth
And touched the stones of Majdanek,
The stones that had no names.
And stroking his beard, he sang his exile's dirge,
The same he sang for thousands of years
From the shores of the rivers of Babylon
To the shores of the Baltic Sea.

Tell Me, Dear Rabbi

Raise your heavy-lidded eyes
And speak to me, dear Rabbi.
Lift your bushy brows, and while you speak,
Nod your head in cadence,
Comb your ageless beard,
Twirl your locks beside your ears,
Speak, all your words revered.

Recount the well-known legendary tale
Engraved in stone by monsoon-carried grains of sand
And by a goose quill drawn on parchment skin.
Tell me of men, of river men, of desert men,
Of pruning hooks and plowshare men,
Of those who dwelled on arid lands.

Tell me again of sin and profanation,
Of Jeroboam the idolater, the worshipper of golden calves,
Of his rebelliousness and wantonness.
And how the Lord, provoked, gave vent to His celestial ire
And punished those he once selected as his own
By covenant to be as many as the grains of sand.

He punished them, you say,
For Father's sins be visited upon his kin
Without forgiveness, without mercy.
And so they trudged along the dusty roads,
Lashed by their Babylonian overlords,
With none to quench their thirst and none to soothe their pain.

Well did they know the road to Babylon,
Once walked by Abraham, the man from Ur,
In search of land and pasture for his kine,
For a new God that claimed to be
The one, the only one,
The God of love and infinite compassion.

And so they walked the exile's road,
God's chosen lot, they walked and wept,
Leaving behind their ruined homes,
Their daughters ravaged, sons enslaved,
Jerusalem reduced to rubble.

The temple an inferno and many dead.
Speak to me, dear Rabbi,
For once upon a time I too had walked
The exile's bitter road,
Jeered by my fellow man and lashed.
I also gazed upon my ruined home
And at the carnage of the many whom I loved.

Was it God's punishment for all my father's sins?
What nature their debauchery?
Did they too worship Anu, Ishtar, Marduk?
Did they too chant the magic incantations?
What were their pagan rites
That so enraged their mountain God?

Have they not prayed or fasted long enough,
Refused assistance to the poor,
Not comforted the orphans,
Denied shelter, bereft of homes,
Taken God's name in vain?

Come, my dear rabbi,
Whose pious name I bear,
Tell me the riddle of my exile.
Unravel the enigma of their sins
So great to warrant punishment, so harsh—
Auschwitz, Sobibor, Belzec, Majdanek.

Or could it be that all is legend,
Crime, punishment, God's wrath, his mercy,
All causes, all effects, mere chance,
For it is man, not God, that metes the lash,
The sea that floods the earth, the sun that burns the seed?
Come, my dear namesake, bend your wise old head.

Rend our clothes, dear Rabbi,
As I have rent my heart.
Come sit next to me and pray
On a humble stool of sorrow,
And let us shed our tears today.

The Echo Man

I am the echo man.
My face is made of stone,
My voice, reverberations,
The sound, an undertone
Of granite bouncing back.

Mutely I stand vigil,
Along with other echo stones,
And wait, surrounded by the sands of time,
For sounds to drift my way.

The echoes come of dreams,
Unwanted in a night,
When past and present,
In a danse macabre entwined,
The dreamers muttering in fright.

I hear the newborn's cry,
Insisting to be loved,
Its manifesto, bill of rights,
The father's pride, the mother's joy.

The echoes come at night,
The whimpering, the cry,
An infant thirsting for its mother's breast,
A mother's whisper of delight.

The sound of schoolboys' shuffling gait,
Reluctant to go to their morning class,
The barking dog, the milkman's call,
The home run cheers,
The night watchman's martial stride.

The solemn organ hymn,
Gloria Patri, et Filio, et Spiritui Sancto,
The bride with blushing cheek,
The trembling hand, the golden ring,
A song of praise, and rice descending from the sky.

Whispers of lovers in each other's arms,
Of solemn promises, I do,
In the beguiling oaths of forever,
In the belated sighs of rue.

An old man's limp,
The cane's staccato beat,
The midnight unexpected ring,
The ticking of the clock, the chime.

I am the echo man without a voice my own.
My granite molecules receiving sound,
Deep etched by winds of time.
Mute witness to the trials of man,
I am the chronicle in pantomime.

They say that in the end all echoes die,
Dwindle, join others, fade
Out there, where silence of eternity,
The graveyard of all sound,
Stands ready to receive, ready for decay.

I say it isn't so,
For I believe that somewhere
In that realm of Milky Ways,
The echoes meet again and sort themselves
By sound, by volume, and content.

And thus reborn, reshaped, resound once more,
And those, attuned to cosmic sounds,
And unbeknown from where they came,
Will listen to the past and forge them into now.

The Mythmaker

I am the maker of myths,
Conjured up in pain and fright,
Things that should have taken place,
Things born in terror and flight.

I am the teller of imaginary tales.
Silently I nurse a tune none ever heard,
A half-remembered melody,
And when the day bows to the night,
The words of joy turn into sorrow.

At times I am the jester,
The grinning circus clown,
My wig, the ashes once upon a time,
A sackcloth is my gown.
My painted tears do taste of salt.

I am the conjurer of myths,
Undoing with a sleight of hand,
With laughter, but at times with tears,
Of days long vanished
And of brooding nights.

Echoes and Cobwebs

It was a steel-fisted time,
When merriment was banned,
And yet she smiled,
Her sighs mistaken for a ditty,
Pagliacci weeping while the audience gaped.

The echoes of her children's songs
Waft through the cobwebs
On a barrack's windowpane,
An empty carriage, a broken rattle,
One eye missing from a raggedy doll,
A lullaby punctured by a cry.

And there were others with her
In a fenced-in barrack,
Reclining on a bloodstained bunk,
A tattered blanket, an empty bowl,
Ruth, Esther, scribbled on a wall.

She longed to be buried in a tattered shroud,
To be mourned when mourning was taboo,
And weeping was the idiom of the day,
And all that was left was stillness,
A time of sorrow for the many slain.

Forgiveness

Go, beat your chest in mea culpa,
The halfway house of self-reproach.

Here you are the judge, no jury here
To nod their heads, perhaps to smile
Or gaze at you with cold disdain or a tearful eye.
You sit alone, no witnesses,
An empty courtroom your domain.

You were the one who wrote the code of law.
You set the date of your nocturnal trials.
You are the one who called the season night,
While others only saw a mundane day
And called it just another war.

Without a robe, naked you stand.
Perplexed, you cast for help,
None but your shadow there.
Is it a trial, a much repeated sham
Born of remorse of deeds beyond recall?

And in that never-ending trial,
You may forgive yourself,
Immerse and cleanse you whole,
Wash the stains of your misdeeds
In all the holy waters of your soul.

And yet, as long as you must dream,
A victim of that long-forgotten night
Compelled to live and live again
The days of anguish, days of blight,
A sad refrain.

An Ode to the Moon

Come, opalescent, languorous moon,
Half-lit, yet promising
To be full-faced to prettify
With your anemic face,
The nightly sky.

Come, come, you solitary pearl
Among the diamond glitter
Of countless stars.
None shine their light as well as you.
None grace the sky.
None rise and wane.

While others sleep,
Braced by their nocturnal dreams,
I, the insomniac, lie awake
With restless limbs,
Waiting to meet you, pallid visitor,
My tryst, my nightly rendezvous.

You're there, the silver pumpkin,
Orion stars your steeds,
And in the nightly sky,
You clear the crest of my imaginary hill
And paint the lea
With luminescent dye.

You rise above horizons
Like Aphrodite emerging from the sea
Majestically, befitting princesses and queens.
You rise, and one by one you shed your veil
To dance the dance of Salome,
To float across the starlit firmament,
A mirror lamp suspended in the sky.

I greet you, lady in the moon,
Faithful companion of my travail.
You were there at night
While gazing at the fenced-in world
And flooding all with silver rays.

Erase the gory sight.
Remember me and all
The beriberi-stricken tots,
Suckling at their mothers' breasts,
Round-bellied, sunken-eyed, the barren earth
A man-made death, man-made decay,
When Eden was a man-made hell.

Do you recall the many nights
The barracks shrouded in a fog
While you, suspended between wire strands,
Cast upon us your milky glare,
Wrapped in some cloudy wands
To hide your tearstained face?

Recall the belching chimneys,
The human ashes wafting in the air.
You must have heard the victims' screams
When Satan's laughter reached your ears.
You must have wept each night.

Today you go on casting silver threads,
Forgotten now, and each and every night
You're there, you fickle traveler,
You with your grinning smile,
Moved by the pendulum of time,
And I am there obediently each night.

Shine on, you temptress,
The bearer of reflected light.
Your striptease act, each month, a quarter moon
To whet our appetite before you shed your lunar garb
And stand there naked to our wanton eyes.
Then slowly, teasingly, you don your clothes again.

There are some men who call themselves with pride
The people of the rising sun,
But I have faith in you, the lady of my nightly tryst,
For you were there in your disguise
When night was balsam to the day.
Each time I gaze at you I swoon,
And so I shall forever be
The man of the rising moon.

Weep Silently

I am afraid to weep,
Lest my lamentations rouse
The sleeping God of vengeance
And his twin companion,
The God of black despair.

Twin Gods,
Their sustenance is tears.
The weeping of the helpless
Is music to their ears.
And dirges nourish them.

And so malevolence thus spawned
Becomes the scorpion's sting
Against the self, the deadly virus,
The bitterness against all men.

So by and by I let them slumber,
Let them be lulled by my deception,
By my falsetto songs,
My painted smile, my imitation grin.

Let Us Remember

Recall the path that led
To where at last we stood.
The softly whispered words
Were meaningless and bland.

Remember them,
When I was John and you were Jane,
Our past a lullaby,
A song's refrain.
While smiling at a blade of grass,
Cease counting our years.

Thoughts to Be Free

My words, twins of my thoughts,
Inking lines on bleached pulp,
Cling from being torn,
Erased, and blown away.

Shadowy, obscure to passersby,
For locked are the gates to my dreams,
Counterfeit words to the casual eye,
None can fathom their meaning.

Only I can feel their anguish,
Their clamoring to be free.

My Poland

My Poland, my Poland,
The land of unrepentant dreamers,
Of those who dreamed and still go on dreaming,
Of those whose dreams were extinguished
By the stroke of a pen of a few
And by men I thought I knew.

My Poland, my Poland,
The land of primrose plains
And bumblebees in clover,
Of northern seas and mountain peaks,
The wafting song of rosemary in bloom,
Of moonlit dreams I knew.

My Poland, my Poland,
Where I drank my mother's milk,
Sweet, at other times so tart,
So sparing and unwillingly conveyed,
And yet I drank to quench my thirst,
The only milk I ever knew.

In dingy rooms and splintered benches
I singsong studied the *aleph-beit*,
In summer heat or chill of northern winds
And on my schoolboy's palm I felt
The taskman's hand and rod
That knew how to punish, and how to soothe
The only hand I knew.

My Poland, my Poland,
Where some danced the Mazur
While we swept the dusty streets,
The sons of Piast and Abraham,
Together we marched in an uneasy gait,
The only gait I knew.

For most of us the dreams had ceased,
Extinguished by a henchman's ax,
While friends of mine in their farewell
Stood at the exit gate,
Brandishing brooms and garbage pails,
The only friends I knew.

The Labyrinth

I dream again:
I lean against the trunk of a ponderosa pine,
Content to read the hieroglyphics of its bark,
Then, turning paths of life's labyrinthine trails,
The chronicles of many years gone by.

I read, I travel back and find myself
Groping anew through many paths of yesterday,
Some dark, forbidding, steeply leading uphill,
My burden, a Sisyphean rock upon my heart.

Paths, doom infested,
Odd specters lurking in the shade,
Others sunlit, bathed with light,
A sea and golden sand.

There on the right I see a path,
Strange, forbidding, beyond recall,
Uncharted and unfathomed in its dread,
One that I fear above all.

I trudge along
And choose the other path,
For in the distance I can hear
The rippling brook and singing of a lark.

Enough of gloom, enough of the night,
All dreams come to an end.
Once darkness sweeps away,
The sun will rise.

The squirrels—merry clowns—
Will pirouette upon the ground,
The butterflies aflutter,
And warblers surely will sing.

And now, just one more turn,
Another exit gate not far away,
I have no choice, a dreamer's plight,
Compelled I must go on and on.

Modern Poetry

To speak,
To write,
Is to be cool,
Far-out, hip, mod,
But far from poetic.

To fly without wings,
To swim without fins,
To walk without limbs,
To write without quills.

To sing without a tune,
Fiddle without a bow,
Beat a drum that has no skin,
Till the earth without a hoe.

So let me be old hat,
Old-fashioned and passé,
Old-fogyish, moss-grown,
Gray-bearded, formal,
And speak with words outworn.

For words, close kin to music,
The idioms of our dreams,
Were made to quicken the heart,
Stir legs to hop, to dance,
Itch palms to clap, and feet to tap.

For words were meant to be the nimble wings,
To lift the heart in daring flight,
Far, far beyond its vocal sway,
And let our word-born souls alight,
To be the vagabonds of each and every day.

The Garden Call

I step into my garden, heeding a summons
Only my ears can perceive.
Was it the infant's cry of thirst
Of my just planted rhododendrons?
Or the parched throats
Of my capricious trees?

I go there, called by voices
In a language strange, unknown,
The song of a bumblebee.
Only I can vaguely perceive
With the skin of my eyes,
The membranes of my ears.

I sit upon a rough-hewn stone,
Planted at random
By fire Gods beneath my feet,
And listen to the melody
Played by the flutter of a fallen leaf
Or by the wing of a costumed butterfly.

Soft music, vaguely perceptible,
Drifts across the fragrant, seed-laden soil,
The whisper of a million reedy stems,
Of wild oats swaying on the slopes,
Bowing in unison to the salty wind,
The song, a promise of another day.

I listen to their tune
Of eons, as yet unknown,
Unknown to me, to other men,
Of days gone by, of days to come,
Of days we shall be one,
The earth, the seed, and I.

Sepia

I have forgotten the softness of your lips,
The velvet caress of your fluttering hand,
The quiver in your voice,
The sigh in asking
When I will return.

You stood at the door,
Clutching at my sleeve,
Sending me away,
Yet wanting me to stay,
Your tears disguised by a smile.

Your eyes, dear Malkale, these I recall.
Through sepia prints they gaze at me,
Full of abandon, full of fear,
Wanting to know yet knowing full well
How many fled, how few came back.

You wore a black shawl on that parting day.
Was it to ward off the cold?
Or was it in readiness to mourn?

I look at the dog-eared sepia print,
Timeworn, a souvenir of who you were.
I ran that day, dear Malkale,
That day I left alone,
And to this day I weep and wonder why.

To Cast a Net

I am a fisherman of faces,
At sail in a turbulent sea.
Even when I have plenty,
I cast my sturdy net
For the sheer pleasure
Of delighting a fisherman's catch,
Then throw them back without regret.

I fish with a bait of longing
For faces lost in the stream of time,
Of passersby once seen, then gone,
The stern, the menacing, those with a frown,
Those flushed with passion, the smiling clown,
And those who've forgotten how to smile.

I fish for faces I once clutched
With a child's grasping hands,
With greedy eyes of the dreaming boy,
A craving gaze of a youth on the go,
With coveting eyes of a greedy man.
I dream of faces I wish were mine.

I fish for those who passed away,
Who disappeared before their time,
Without a farewell kiss, without good-bye,
A fleeting glimpse, a train afar,
Their footprints long erased by tears.

With lure in hand I gaze
Upon the waves of days gone by,
My fishing rod, my hands a bit unsteady now.
The faces are still there,
Concealed within the waves of my recall,
Cherubic some or prematurely aged.

At sunset I gaze upon my catch
And gently throw them back
Into the seas of years gone by.
I throw them one by one,
And parting, bid them, *"Mon ami, adieu,"*
"Hasta la vista," "Arrivederci," until we meet again.

Melancholy Days

They come, unbidden actors,
To recite unbidden lines
Upon a bleak and gloomy stage,
And only I, the only audience there.

The curtains rise,
My winged and lofty thoughts,
Like ravens take to flight
At nearness of a plowman's blade,
And vanish into dimness of the coming night.

The footlights dim, and night floods the stage,
The birds of song retreat within the canopies of trees,
New wings begin to fill the sky,
The denizens of caves, the flitting bats of days gone by.

With webbed wings between their toes,
They come on their nocturnal flight.
They come by stealth,
Too shy to show their faces by day.

With weary eyes I see the actors now,
Stripe-suited, walk in rows of five.
Shadowy they trod across the stage,
Their feet in clogs,
Their legs in prison chains.

They walk their shuffling gait
With spindly legs and spindly arms,
Their hollow eyes fixed at the rutted lane,
Behind them prison gates,
Ahead, perhaps another day.

One of them staggers, too weak to go on.
He stumbles. Then he falls.
The snarling watchdogs bark.
The helmeted guard readies his gun.

"Please, *bitte, nein, gevalt*
Pozhaluysta, shema," he pleads.
"I shall not fall again."
The shot rings just the same.

Another falls, another dies,
And many more.
None ever hears their cries.
The column shorter
Treads on across the stage.

And I, attending audience of only one,
Stagger along with them again, again,
As I have done before
On far-off roads,
Concealed from human eyes.

The stage has dimmed,
And in my front row seat,
My legs move silently with theirs,
While one by one they die
And I sit there alive, and weep.

And so they die.
I mourn them, yet I live to sing
Under the merciful shadow
Of an eagle's wing
And often wonder why.

The Exile's Serenade

Rejoice, my fellow émigrés,
The banished, ostracized,
Expelled by fellow men,
Excluded, shunned,
Now aliens in this land.

Once we were banned, outlawed
For speaking with a single mind
Against stale customs.
Harbingers of modern times,
We dared the eagles and the flags.

Don't weep, my fellow exiles,
Go raise your head with pride,
You wandering, downtrodden Jews of old,
Unwanted lepers, Ishmaels,
The men beyond the pale.

Go, bid adieu, good-bye, farewell
To old familiar shores,
To dingy huts, to barren fields, and narrow lanes.
Now is the time to wipe your tears
And cease to gaze at what you left behind.

For exile is as old as man,
Starting with Adam and his curious Eve.
Like them we have transgressed,
Our sins, the thirst to know,
The Eden too restrained.

We sinned for speaking out.
When silence was the language of the land,
We dared to walk when men
Like serpents slithered on the ground
And walked with heads bowed down.

We spoke of peace,
While others killed and maimed.
We spoke of love,
While others fumed with hate.
We healed the sick. We prayed.

So kick your heels and dance
Your polka, waltz, the tarantella,
The polonaise, mazurka,
Your hopak and bourrée.

Go, stomp your feet, and clap your hands.
Be bold, be not afraid.
Come brace my waist and dance with me,
And sing the exile's serenade.

The Sculptor

None ever showed him how to carve,
And yet the knives, led by a reverent hand,
Keenly knew her hidden shape,
Her asking to be free, unbound.

And so he worked, the wooden block braced in his arms,
The chisels and the gouges stirred to life,
Telling him how deep to cut,
How smoothly to caress, how much to shave.

The pace-setting mallet would halt in midair
To slow the all-too-eager hand,
Or speed the cutting rate when faltering,
Afraid to cut, to wound the wooden grain.

Her shoulder came in sight,
The bride disrobed, he once caressed,
Smooth then and alabaster white,
Her neck atilt, ashamed to meet her lover's eyes.

Her head, once held so high,
Was now concealed, her chin between her breast,
Weeping in deep sorrow for her only child,
Supine and lifeless in her lap.

How bent her back, how flail her arms,
Resigned and limply hanging at her side,
Strands of her hair
Cascading down the side of her bowed head.

She lost her child.
They took it from her on a day
When Gods mistook the day for night
And killing firstborns was in season once again.

He wasn't there to wipe her tears.
He wasn't there to press their child against his breast.
He wasn't there to brace her later on,
When she no longer could endure and joined their child.

At last his trembling chisel cut her free.
No longer captive to his dream,
He saw her now, the way he knew
She must have looked
The day her world came to an end.

The Kite

I was a child, a kite,
Forever in pursuit of eddies in the air,
Caressed by the wind,
The past behind me,
A ballast to be tossed without a care.

I flew with restless wings and longed
For all my sunsets to give rise to dawn,
The nights to a be abridged,
My daydreams, gilded links with those to come.

With lofty speed
I fought the currents of my times,
The morals and the customs of my day,
My foes, all those who disagree.

The tail, the rudder in the current of my flight,
The guiding hand of precedent,
Was showing me that all tomorrows start today.
Each sunset has its dawn.

Then came a day of sad recall.
I gazed behind me and wondered why
The past, the tail end of my kite,
Trailing behind, was in pursuit of me.

A part of me—it was still there
And wagging joyously—
Was telling me that kites without their tails
Could never fly, will falter, sway.

Rained upon, the fibers frayed,
The skin no longer taut,
Less avidly to catch the currents of the air,
I fluttered and I sighed.

Scorched by the burning heat,
Made brittle by the icy wind,
I slowed my flight, too cautious now,
For there ahead of me I saw the dusk
And just beyond the night.

And down below me
In the autumn wilted hills, the dales, the leas,
Were other kites with tattered wings,
Timeworn, their tails inert as mine.

The Past

The past slinks right behind me,
A cat in sly pursuit of mice,
A hungry lion on the prowl,
The midnight tide beckoned by the rising moon,
The past—my shadow, even on a sunless day.

Angry for being forgotten,
It comes, with the howl
Of a gale-whipped autumn day,
Lashing the lands, lashing the sea.
It comes demanding to be heard.

Or it slinks silently,
A mute beggar with a stretched-out hand,
The seagull soaring with a listless wing,
The midnight waves at rest and calm,
The prowling owl at night.

And even then, on quiet days,
I dare not turn my head to look
At the unbidden guest
Intruder on my ease.

The past, my deeds and my misdeeds,
Those of my hands, those done to me,
Bloodshed and barbed wire days.

I wish to part from them,
To cast them far away,
A reptile molting of its skin,
A tree about to shed its autumn leaves,
A flock of birds on their autumn flight.

But it is only futile wishing.
My mime, the shadow of things past, is there.
No sponge can wash it off.
No sleight of hand, no magic can erase
My anchor stone, a burden I must wear.

Of Music

In a dream I pull the bow
In a legato, even glide
Across the cello strings, and they resound
In antiphonal chant with
A longing of a distant time.

And as I play, I see my girl
Sit on an abandoned log
Along the bank of a swift stream,
And in the wind caressing her,
I hear the echo of my song.

I listen to the notes,
Each one a prelude to the next,
Each one a flourish for a tune.
I used to sing
While young and free of care.

And suddenly my bow
Changed pace, the dulcet tune,
Sweet-flowing, rich, and mellow,
Gives way to a discordant sound,
A slur, a minor key, a dissonance.

For there approaching her I see a man—
No, not a man, a boy, my closest friend—
And with a swagger he comes near
And puts his arm around her waist
And fervently embraces and kisses.

With trembling arm, I draw the bow,
The song, a melody of wrath,
Of burning rage, and how I wish
The bow to be a dagger in my hand,
A tool to punish, even up the score.

Sated with their shameless kisses,
They turn around and look at me
With challenge in their eyes,
And realizing who they are,
I cast the dream away.

I nod my head and silently I smile.
The fragrant wood against my chest
Caresses me again.
The bow, extension of my hand,
Sings dulcet notes against the strings,
A harmony of chords.

And I awaken with a smile,
For now I realize
That she is she, all right,
And my pernicious friend,
My deadly foe,
Is no one else but I.

A Ballad of McCreary

His father drowned when he was three.
His mother was a fishwife in some port
And then abandoned him for some strange man,
And like so many others of his clan,
He too became an orphan of the sea,
His nursemaids rawboned tars
The rolling deck his swing.

And so he grew into a mighty lad,
Casting his fisherman's nets
Wider and swifter than any other man.
They called him McCreary,
The best one in his clan.
Each setting day he brought in his haul,
He grew into a legend, an envy of them all.

He is an old man now, McCreary,
Hunched over in his skiff,
His hand still resting on the till,
Coarse-wrinkled, windswept, stiff,
Age-cracked, sea-burned his skin,
His tired eyes unblinking, staring
At the setting sun at each day's end.

Day after day he sits,
Watching the lapping waves
Against the prow, the keel, and aft,
Soft-resting in the sand
On a shore that bears no name,
The splintered mast a spar,
A tattered sail, a knotted rope.

The old sailor, deaf now,
Deaf to the concertina at the inn,
The drunken hollering for ale or gin,
The sailors' briny songs,
And yet his ears are still attuned
To the roar of the endless sea,
The screeching of the gulls and terns.

He can no longer hear
The ringing of the harbor bell,
Though sea breezes buffeting the sails
Still reach his muted ear.
"Ahoy there!" echoes from afar.
The roaring waves of the stormy sea
Accompany his nightly dreams.

And now he waits, old man McCreary,
For the tides to carry him to sea,
For, from the sea he came,
And there he must return.
It was once his nursemaid,
Mistress, and his chum.
He waits for her to take him back,
And in her bracing swells
McCreary wishes to succumb.

The Seasons

I still recall
The time when men and women
Spoke with silken lyre strings,
Their heads adorned by halos,
The sweet quenching of my thirst,
The soft swaddling of their hands.

Their words, embraces,
Whispers of compassion,
Touching softly, soothingly,
Each song a lilt,
My father's chant an incantation.

Then came the storm,
With shadows of a crooked cross,
And smiles gave way to lamentation.

When Torah scrolls went up in flames,
The cantor's chants a wail,
The sacraments a whisper,
And church bells rang in mute incomprehension,
And those he loved were gone,
Never to return.

One day I was alone,
Freed of his shackles.
I wept, bewildered by the change,
As yet unsure. Was it the end,
Or was it the commencement
Of a day I couldn't fully comprehend?

Illusions

Adrift between wakefulness and sleep,
I stopped at the threshold.
Afraid to meet the commonplace of day,
I longed to dream
And thus became creator of another realm.

Imitating Yahve, I cast the light
Upon the unlit earth,
Illumined the eternal sky,
Set the moon spinning in its orbit.

Then cleaved the seas to bring forth
Headlands, bluffs, and hills,
The wind-born birds,
The fish, their gills,
The swells, the tides, the rushing brooks—
I gazed at it, sighed, and called it swell.

I threw the seeds upon the fecund land,
The trees upon the hills, the orchids on their limbs,
The flowers, fruits, and grains, I made them sprout,
Invented wilt, decay, then birth again,
The stork upon a perch,
The roaring lion in its den.

At last to entertain myself, I fashioned man
To crawl, then strut upon the earth,
An angel without wings.
And with a thunderous voice I spoke to him,
Through brambles and a burning bush.
"Take off your shoes," I said, "and bow your head."

Then lit the spark of passion in his loin,
He asked for Eve and asked for sons,
And so I did and thought it good again.
Then, tired of my earthly work,
I rested on my Sabbath day.

And in that garden of my toil, I heard a cry,
Two brothers, prototypes of man,
One with a jealous heart, the other slew,
Then hid before my eyes.
I heard no lament, saw no remorse,
Only defiant greed to know,
Heeding the serpent and not my laws.
And so I exiled them,
My guardian angel with his flaming sword,
Barring the way from ever coming back.
And then I looked at my misdeeds
And fled from being God.
I chose to be an ordinary man again.

And so I drew the curtain on my dream,
Let darkness rule upon the land,
Let genesis be Yahve's deed.
If murder and deceit be acts of God,
I'd rather be a dreamless, bungling,
Simple man, a clod.

Homecoming

She came home with cautious steps,
As yet unsure of being well.
I see the pallor of her skin,
The drooping eyelids stemming tears,
Both hers and mine.

The empty hollow in the pillow
For so many days is filled again.
The wind whispers on the slanted roof,
Soft whispers of her sleeping at my side,
And full of gratitude I stay awake.

A Letter to My Colleagues

Tell me, Herr Kollege,
My dear colleague clad in white,
Where in days gone by,
When studiously you listened with a solemn brow,
To your patient's plea for life.

Where had you been, dear colleague,
When they shaved my head,
Tattooed my soul, shackled my legs
With barbed wire,
Then set a lock upon my lips,
And starving me, tried to extinguish
The memory that I was man?

When they murdered my children, one by one,
Then all the others that I loved,
While you, disciples of a madman's thirst for death,
Your carnage men who killed for lust
Marched on with glee to Satan's drumbeat tune.
What others built they churned to dust.

Willingly you joined the jeering crowd,
With cheeks aflame you too had raised your arm,
The "Heil," your new salute,
The language, a staccato beat,
Your songs, a hymn to death,
Your symphonies upon a time,
Now songs of war.

Frenzied with killing you failed to see
The clouds of burning flesh blotting the sky,
The ashes of millions scattering upon your fields,
Your ears turned deaf to the anguished cry
Of those reciting Te Deum, *Shema*, while victims
Begged to be allowed to live another day.

A vengeful God, you chose to rule,
Obediently you followed his ukase.
Blithely you signed certificates
Of the infirm, the destitute, the lame,
Those of a different faith,
Those of a different thought.

Your ears turned deaf to children's cries.
First you burned books; then you burned men.
And in your ignorance you burned your children's souls,
And in that witches Sabbath,
In ignorance of who you really were,
You killed the best you ever had,
Along with those of us who wished you well.

Our thoughts, beyond your grasp,
Our words mere whispers none could hear,
I and the multitudes whose lives you ravished,
Whose lands you blistered, scorched,
Were left to curse you and your misbegotten kin,
Heap maledictions on your breed between our sobs,
Accusing you of every sin.

Were you asleep then, Herr Kollege?
Were you so overcome, so overwhelmed
By the resounding drumbeat of your time?
Was it amnesia of your heart?
Sleep now, my fellow healers, sleep well.

Horst Wessel Song

Doff your hats, salute your *Heil,*
Step on the sidewalk, make room, *mach Frei,*
For there come marching men in brown,
Singing in unison their *"Eins, zwei, drei."*

They march, their boots
Beating the rhythm, the drums,
Twin sounds of martial tunes,
Galloping sounds of apocalyptic steeds.

They sing of flags held high,
Of glistening bayonets tinged with a Jew's blood,
Of sacrifice, of bloody rites,
Of glory, *"Ein Volk, ein Reich, ein Führer."*

The tune an alien
Storm of sounds, a dissonance
Made to incite and to arouse in man
The lust for death and blight.

They sing, the new anthem,
The song a call to kill, to maim.
Born of Horst Wessel, a thug, a pimp,
The new order's hero man.

"Die Fahnen hoch," they march
While those of us without a friend
Stand mute, despairingly alone,
And others deaf to our despair.

An Old Sailor's Song

I am too old to love
With raging passion,
A storm-whipped sea,
A lion's strength in my embrace.

My passion now, the gentle breeze at dawn,
The morning dew, the promise
Of the sun to clear the mountain crest,
The pledge of yet another day.

Soft labor now my daily toil,
The sun had set once more,
My sails are lashed,
While calmly I steer my way to shore.

Home I return to seek repose,
To gaze upon the blue calmed sea,
To watch the sun depart,
The evening star to laud the night.

Walk down the path, beloved mine,
Come into my arms,
Look not askance
At my tired face, my snow-white hair.

Tonight let us embrace
Before too late.
Let the past years take flight,
And once more be my lassie,
My ever-loving bride.

70

My Purple Iris

With awe I look upon your bloom,
One of the first to grace the winter beds,
Your cousins, freesias, crocuses, and glads,
Still dreaming in their lair,
Still warming their half-frozen limbs,
Waiting to stretch their tendrils to the air.

On a refreshing April day,
You came with swordlike leaves,
Piercing the virgin crust of earth,
Stretched to the skies,
Still harboring the tender stalk,
The newborn blossom swaddled like a child.

Born of a rhizome, you emerge in twos or threes,
Shy at first on tender limbs,
Enfolded in your purple dress,
Reluctant to display as yet
Your purpureal nakedness,
Plum-purple proud and pansy violet.

The winter gusts have ceased,
The drumroll rays of spring your music,
To disrobe yourself,
Flirtatiously unfold the lacy falls,
The collarets, the stamens,
Your diadems, your royal crown.

Dappled and striate, made to allure
The butterfly, the ever-thirsty hummingbird,
You shed your leafy wrap,
You pompous purple stripper enticingly unclad,
Regal and majestic,
The mantle like a peacock's tail.

They named you Iris, you alluring dame,
The goddess of the rainbow.
Are you a queen in a purple robe,
The consort of a king to rule supreme?
Or are you on a masquerade,
A monsignor, the purple bishop's mantel your disguise?
Or are you just to please my eyes?

The Buccaneer of Lincoln High

You braved the stormy seas.
A gale had snapped the mast.
Your shipmate, your best friend,
Into the raging waves was cast.

You are the strutting buccaneer,
Tarrying in harbors of exotic lands,
Of half-clad damsels, almond eyes,
Shrill whistles, tambourines, and wailing chants.

At last, with tattered sails,
You're home again after so many years,
The salty breeze still in your hair,
The echo of the hurricane still in your ears.

Put back the rapier, buccaneer,
Into the gem-encrusted scabbard.
Desist now from your infamous career.
You're home, past your travails.

Your math homework is still not done,
The garbage pail unemptied by the door,
Your bed unmade, your hair still unkempt,
The school bus on its way.

Come, get your chocolate, for it is late.
You're safe now, Mama's gangly buccaneer.
You've dueled, and you've killed.
It's over now, intrepid musketeer.

And cease to frown your acned brow,
For there are seven seas as yet to sail,
A million men to match your blade,
Mountains galore for you to scale.

And so much time is left,
Intrepid buccaneer,
So dream and dream, and while you do
You better hurry up, the bus is here.

There Was a Time

There were days to remember,
Days full of darkness, the sun eclipsed by fear,
When men, trying to see,
Had to avert their gaze,
Days of alarm, days of dismay,
Death using the palette of death to paint itself
With the facsimile of men.

I try to erase them, trample on,
Burn the unwanted pages,
The calendar of all too many days,
Turn a mute ear to the harsh sounds,
And listen only to the harmony of song.

To look at faces and be blind
To all the scars there etched
By acid of the many tears,
Shed by so many, some vanished now,
And all those left behind.

The World Is a Stage

The world is a stage,
And we, unwitting actors
In our life's allotted time,
Strut back and forth,
Gesturing, reciting in prose or rhyme
By means of words, by means of song,
By signals, or by pantomime.

At times I was compelled to watch the play,
Allotted to a front row seat.
Agog and full of wonder did I gaze,
But there were times when troubled by the glare
Of the bright floodlights,
The hullabaloo, the loud fanfare,
I sought a seat way in the rear,
Along with others overcome by fright.

Some in the audience clapped,
Others hooted, some even cheered,
A catcall here and there,
Some dared to hiss, some even wept,
And to this day, aghast by what I saw,
I keep on wondering with pity and dismay
Who was the playwright
And why this gory play.

To My Heirs

To you
I bequeathed the throb of my heart,
The depth of my breath,
My temper, and my calm.

I gave you my shape,
My face, demeanor, pride,
The mettle to endure,
The feebleness to fail.

To praise when all went well,
At other times to chide,
As someday you in turn
Will do the same.

And like the never-changing tide,
Its ebb and flow,
We all receive and then bestow
The gist of who we are.

The Newcomer

Swathed, bundled up, tightfisted, it arrives,
The hairless bundle of pink flesh,
Forever thirsty, suckling, screaming at full throat.
Cross-eyed, it squirms in our arms,
And we, agog, call it the great hope.

You wanted me, it seems to say.
Was it a carnival, a spree of lust,
A drunken revelry, a feast of love?
Too late, it says, it matters not,
Now take me as I am.

The Chase

He was a boy with scabs on his knees,
With unkempt hair and running nose,
Smudges of dirt tattoos on his chin,
Scuffed shoes, his pants too short.

His pockets bulged with marbles,
Dried chestnuts, flat pebbles,
A piece of twine, a twisted nail,
A treasure trove of magic rings.

Smooth river-polished bits of glass,
A slingshot with one broken tine,
A pocketknife with half a blade,
An unripe apple, a stolen plum.

He was a boy with wings,
Full of disdain to walk.
He took to the air with every step,
Carried aloft by the wind.

A champion catcher of pollywogs
And other crawling things,
He wrestled lions,
Chased eagles in the sky.

And then one day the boy was on the run,
Chased by a man with silver hair,
A limping man, brandishing a cane,
Waving his arm, gasping for a bit of air.

A dreamer man, he too was on the run,
Pursuing the boy he once had been,
Pursuing and yelling with a faltering voice,
"Wait for me, my boy, please wait."

"Once I was you," he shouted from afar.
"Oh, let me be the boy again.
Please, let me be the boy you are,
If only for a single day."

To Worship

Men worshipped God, who spoke to them
From a mountaintop in the wilderness of Shem,
God's voice, the burning bush,
Commandments etched in stone
By the desert-swirling sands.

And in the shadow of a tree
There sat a man,
A former nobleman, a loincloth now his garb,
Hands resting in his lap,
And on his lips an enigmatic smile.

He spoke from the top of a pyramid,
Steps crimson with his victim's blood,
His priests in gilded gowns,
Disguised half canine and half men,
The gilded serpent as their crowns.

One spoke with the knell of thunder,
Another with the roar of the sea,
Or in the icy chill of the northern wind,
Some form the lofty Mount Olympus
Or the halls of Valhalla.

Mine spoke to me clad in a prayer shawl,
A man-made tent enfolding him
From head down to his heels,
And I, his grandson, with rapt ear
Could hear the angels sing.

He spoke to me in dulcet tones,
A twinkle in his heavy-lidded eye,
Words muted by a snuff-stained beard,
Words to behold and to live by,
Words near and yet so far away.

His song, a lullaby,
The same his father sang,
A singsong melody of Hebrew lore,
An old refrain, an invocation,
Shalom for peace, not war.

There were times we slowly walked,
The boy beside the peddler man,
A child entrusted to his care.
We walked, he with his weary steps,
Light-footed, buoyant mine.

We walked, we spoke, his words
Gravely autumnal, mine of sweet spring of youth,
Of goodness, virtue, savants, and fools,
Of sins, punishments, rewards,
Of Jacob wrestling with the angels,
Of paupers, righteous men, and ancient bards.

Then came the years of military boots,
Of outstretched arm salutes and shouts,
When arbiters of life and death were only men,
And plowshares fashioned into swords again,
And pruning hooks made into spears.

One day we ceased to walk, the peddler man and I,
Uneasy silence, only nods and frightened stares.
When Satan ruled and angels fled,
Good deeds and virtue hid their face,
And brutal slaughter ruled upon in the land.

Then came a day they took the stooped old man,
And while I wept to see him in a cattle train,
Slit windows and the cries for help,
Barbed wire, little hands aflutter to be free,
Black plumes of smoke blotting out the sky.

One day the winds of murder ceased,
Men, prostrate, genuflecting, swaying once again,
Went on to worship Gods anew,
But I could only see an empty cattle train,
No Gods to walk with, hand in hand.

The Sand

Some spend their lives collecting gems,
Exotic furs, expensive art, rare stamps,
Or desiccated flowers, wilted leaves
Of gone-by ages, ancient times.

I'm a man of sand,
Gathering the dust of time
From where I came,
To where I must return.

The sand, the grit in one man's eye,
The sandbar, sailor's bane at sea,
The sirocco, the khamsin,
The desert traveler's curse,
A weary traveler's snare,
A nature's deadly sleight of hand.

The rushing river sand,
The soft carpet of the seas,
The building particles of land,
The genesis of dales and hills.

The shifting sands of history,
The burial place of kings and queens,
Of long-forgotten realms
And those obeying their commands.

And while I sift the grains
From hand to hand,
I listen to their whisper
Of long-forgotten lands.

With awe I watch the hourglass,
The flow of sand, the man-made flow of time,
The time clock gauge of birth and death,
The teller when to plow and when to reap.

These are my sands,
These I bequeath to you, my son,
For we are all the dust of time,
The shifting particles of life.

Shana Tova 5761

The clock of eons soon shall chime again.
The hand will move one notch upon the face of time,
And facing east, believers will recite,
"Avinu Malkainu," our Lord sublime.
"Al Khait Khutuni," forgive, absolve
The sinners that we are.

Pardon all misdeeds, transgressions.
Bestow on us and all of our kin
Life, prosperity in the year to come,
As you have done before
To us, the people of your covenant.

So pray for me, my friend,
For on this day of reverence,
This holy day of awe,
Beset by darkness of my doubts,
Doubts born of cold despair,
My lips still remain profane.

For I grew deaf,
No longer hear the words of Psalms,
Blind to the ink on parchment scrolls,
Too many died before their time,
Death by the caprice of one's fellow man,
While all the Gods were silent,
Too silent for me to beg, implore.

My Autumn Apple Tree

The winds of a gray autumn
Of melancholy days are near.
The migrant birds have fled.
The earth-born morning mist,
Chilly and inert, fails to lift.

Mourn not, my apple tree,
The bearer of many gifts,
Your leaves turned into butterflies.
Wind-driven, they have come alive
To fly, to land, to rest awhile.
Let's bid them bon voyage
In their autumnal flight.

Weep not, as fluttering they part
In autumn gusts at season's end.
Each tree must let them go
To their retreat, to their repose,
As we must all in time.

'Tis the season, the end of leafy toil,
To join the other butterflies,
Seeking the warm and humid soil,
Season's soft slumber for their wintry night,
A season to dream, to be reborn.

Go stretch your tired limbs,
Shade-giving, fruitful tree.
Unclad, you need your winter sleep
Beneath the eiderdown of snow,
Your branches swaying heavily, and dream,
For soon the balmy winds of spring
Will cause a thousand buds to burst
To greet a newborn sky.

The fragrance of your blooms
Will wake the sleeping bees
Soon to commence their dance,
To sing, to hum, sweet pollen on their wings.
New leaves with sprout, myriad clinging babes,
And you, the mother of them all,
Your limbs, your canopy widespread,
Letting the sun caress their face,
Their sustenance their daily bread.

So rest, you arboreal cornucopia,
You legend tree of paradise,
Your trunk the pillow to the dreamer,
Beneath your boughs a lover's tryst,
Your roots the tendril of the earth,
For in the end we all must heed the night
Before we greet the rising sun.

The Clockmaker

I see him there, bent over wheels and springs
And softly muttering to none.
He mends things,
The many watches, clocks, the pace of time,
The swinging of a pendulum,
The dulcet chime.

He's gone, the man of broken springs,
The sentinel of time,
Who gazed upon me
With a loupe within one eye
And only saw a ticking progeny
In need to mend, to pacify.

A cattle train took him away,
To where so many others went,
Leaving behind his son,
The empty vials of acid and of oil,
The silent clocks upon the wall,
And the forever silenced chimes.

The Immigrants

Come, let us cross the stormy sea.
Let us cross as others did before,
Sails lashed by our dreams,
And hope, our rudder and the oar.

No tearful parting from the lands
Where vengeful Gods reside
On crosses, on gilt spires,
On domed temples with a star.

Where lashes were the daily fare
And where the Star of David,
Once pride upon a warrior's shield,
Became the symbol of despair.

Cease gazing at the heaving sea,
The endless undulating span.
Forget the shtetls, hamlets,
Dingy ghettos, huts, the aging clan.

The thatch, the reeking gutters
Along the rutted village lanes,
The clatter of the peasant carts,
The grunting pigs, the braying ass.

Shipwrecked of heart and mind,
The back-bent poor,
And those too proud to stoop,
And those no longer able to endure.

Ill-clad and shivering you stand,
Clutching the salty rail,
Huddled for warmth
Against the autumn gale.

Remember you were former slaves,
As yet not fully freed,
No chains, no fetters, though,
No iron gates.

Your arms tattooed
With numbers, not with hearts,
Your vision limited, confined
By concrete and barbed wire.

Come taste the wind, the salty brine
Of freedom yet to come,
A freedom yet deferred.

Come now, my shipmates, men of sorrow,
Come, move your tired legs,
Unbend your broken backs.
There is a patch of blue above our heads.

Swing in our hammocks,
Peer into the darkness of the sea,
As yet no castles there,
Only a starry canopy, a heaving sea.

The lady with the torch stands there,
As yet too far away and wrapped in mist.
Like our hopes, she stands at the gate
In tranquil silence, head unbent.

No welcome sign along the shore,
No welcome mat, a steely plank,
An oily concrete ramp,
A dingy hall ahead.

Look, shipmates, at the men in blue and some in gray.
Look at them and soothe your throbbing heart.
You've seen too many men in blue till now,
Too many men with empty stares.

Men, blind to see into your hearts,
To read your thoughts,
Men—only hinges opening the gates
Or closing them once again.

Harsh men and stern,
Men only made to sift, to pry,
Men who forgot their father's blackened face
Of many years gone by.

They gaze without seeing you and want to know
"Yea've somethin' to declare?
Some smuggled goods, some contraband,
Some hanky-panky forgeries, forbidden ware?"

Be silent, tired shipmates,
Don't smile and don't you weep.
He speaks of items to declare—
Your baggage, bundles, duffel bags.

The cherished items lie hidden in your heart,
Invisible, unreadable to all but you.
The time to open them and to declare is years ahead,
When we shall walk like other men
With our heads held high.

To Mourn

For we must mourn them now
Before the chroniclers with crafty pens
Erase that monstrous crime.
Come, let us weep for those whose tears ran dry,
Their voices cast away before their time.

"If I forget thee, O Jerusalem," men wept
Upon a time, bereft of all they lost,
"Let my right hand forget her cunning,
My tongue cleave to the roof of my mouth."
Their monument, a canticle, a prayer's rhyme,
A dirge, a lament to this day.

We cannot stay the hands of time.
Winds and decay will turn to dust,
An obelisk, a crumbling wall, a lofty monument,
And all the tomes, no matter how sublime,
Men will forget, erase, misrepresent.

But while we live, our voices yet undimmed,
Like Rachel weeping for her children,
Let us remember them, for to be silent
Is to join the many, who with diffidence
Watched our children lose their lives
One by one.

Freedom

The ornate gates were sprung, and he was free
To walk away with a wobbly gait,
To wave his spindly arms.
At last he dared to raise his head
To an unblemished summer sky,
To greet the sun, a road ahead,
To let the gentle wind
Caress his ashen face.

And squatting at the river's edge,
He tried to scrub his callous hands.
No soap would cleanse them,
Not even river sands.
None could erase the images
Of pleading arms.

The rippling stream was cool,
Bathing his arms, his legs,
Bearing the imprints of his manacles
Upon his flesh,
The whip so painful and so swift,
The curses and abuse
His jailer's parting gift.

Soft, soothing was the shade,
The canopy of summer leaves
Upon his brow
To reverie, to dream of life,
No longer death, the ever-present guest.
But in his dreams before his eyes,
A hangman's noose.

Autumn

Time slows to the rhythm
Of soft-falling autumn leaves,
To gently swaying poplar trees,
To my tired, shuffling steps
Through the soft wilt
Beneath my feet.

The morning dew paints silvery
The roadside thistle,
The rolling hills, the river stones,
The half-denuded branches
Of a gnarled apple tree.

My ears attuned to songs of yesterday,
I walk and only faintly hear
The melody of autumn winds.
My tired eyes no longer see
The plumage of the birds in flight.

It is the autumn of the day.
It is the autumn of my life,
My days no longer preludes
Of softly breaking dawns,
Days half-forgotten epilogues,
Adrift white river swans.

Of Nature

I never fail to like a tree,
Its shade, the nesting place for birds,
And when abloom in spring
Of nectar-searching bees
With autumn fruit and heavy boughs,
The fragrant leaves
Stoop low to kiss the ground,
A fondling touch upon my face.

I never fail to love a rose in autumn bloom,
Even a wilted one about to shed its leaves
Before its winter sleep,
Their wafting scent carried by the wind,
The autumn-yellowed leaves
A canopy upon the garden bed.

Spellbound, I stand each spring
And watch the irises, their spindly buds,
The pallid, spiky leaves,
The collars and the falls unfold,
A rainbow's gift to lure the eye.

I even like the dandelion,
That wily, sneaky garden weed,
Its pungent yellow bloom, its milky sap,
Wind carried, floating in the air,
A thousand white umbrellas carrying its seed,
To sprout where none would dare.

Oh, yes, I like the flowers and the trees,
And how I wish to say the same
Of Homo sapiens of my creed,
Some of my kin, some neighbor next to me,
Or those who sullenly walk down the street,
Some puffed with pride and full of bigotry.

The Garden

With the hoe in hand,
A song in my breast,
And spring in the air,
I till the fallow soil.
It is my springtime,
My wake-up call for toil.

The springtide morning mist,
Aurora's twilight dawn,
Soft-breaking, almost shy,
Puts the stars to flight,
Caressing the melancholy sky.

The tedious sunless days
Have fled and given way
To sparkling rays.
An avalanche of light rolls down
The mountain slope's incline.

Wan sunshine until now
Is ready to bestow its gifts anew,
The wilted grass upon the hill.
The faded blades of yesterday
Are green again.

There is no crowing of a cock,
No lowing of a cow.
It is the lark, the mockingbird,
To greet the sun,
To swell the pregnant buds,
To let the bees hum once again.

And on such a day of spring,
I till the fallow soil,
With sweat upon my brow,
Creation's legacy upon rebellious man,
His angel with a flaming sword,
Showing the road from paradise to hell.

Defiantly I shake my head,
I swing my hoe and harrow with my rake,
And challenging the angels,
The serpents, and my fate,
I've come back to my garden,
Brandishing my spade,
To live and to reclaim
The sleeping earth again.

Of Sabbath Chants

I hear them sing,
Though their voices have been stilled,
And yet I hear them sing.
The melodies reverberate
Sweet echoes to this day.

These were the songs,
When I was young,
My chants of yesterday,
The only ones I ever knew.

The solemn hymns
Of slowly swaying men,
Dark twilight entering
The unlit, dingy room.

Recitations in a tired voice
By an old man, and I, his child,
Joining with my lilting tune,
A dream and only half awake.

These were my cradlesongs
Of a long, long time ago,
My haunting lullabies,
My reveries and my reality.

Long gone, those chanting men,
The singers swaying back and forth,
Darkly clad, their beards unshorn,
The wide-brimmed hats.

Perished now, forever gone,
But on a Sabbath afternoon
At dusk,
Their plaintive songs still linger on.

To Remember Them

None will remember them.
The tears shed by their sons
In time will cease to flow.
The sorrow finally will end.

The chiseled stones will not withstand
The flaming sun, the burnishing of sand.
The winds will soon erase their names.
Parchments will yellow, crumble, burn.

The thespian's strident voice,
Once droning on the stage,
Will turn to whispers,
Then taper, and then fade.

A children's song,
A fiddler's bow upon a string,
The flicker of a candle,
Then silence—darkness will ensue again.

The hanging gardens of ancient Babylon,
Lighthouses towering upon the sea,
The Mayan temples, ruins now,
Mute witnesses to what they were.

A thousand Gods, those of the sea,
Of fire, and of stone, have come and gone.
Feeble became the scribbler's hand,
His well-honed quill becoming dull.

Vanished now the lecherous king,
Who, with a lyre in his hand,
Sang ruefully his *Shir Hashirim*,
My "Song of Songs."

"Man is like to vanity," he sang,
His days are as a shadow
That passeth away,
His dulcet voice upon a time
Hardly a whisper now.

Reb Shlomo, the Beggar

Welcome, Reb Shlomo,
You mutely stand there at midday,
Stooped, leaning to one side
Like a wind-beaten tree,
Your rugged face, your beard in disarray.

You never smile, Reb Shlomo, never frown.
You enter and silently stand,
Hands hidden in your pockets.
With melancholy eyes you gaze at us,
Without complaint, without reproach.
You never entreat, you never implore.

We know why you are there.
No need for you to speak,
For begging is your trade,
As you proceed from door to door,
Receiving alms, a penny, sometimes more.
You take them as your dues,
Your birthright to receive.

You are no vagabond, Reb Shlomo,
No tramp, no derelict, for in your moral code,
To beg is not a vice, to be a beggar no disgrace,
No burning shame, and no dishonor,
For giving is our noble deed.

With murmured benediction
On your pale and hardly moving lips,
You settle all your debts, indemnify,
Repay in kind, your words, your blessing,
For pennies, in your outstretched hand,
You look upon as fair exchange.

New Year

Soon the bells will ring.
The silver apple will descend.
Those on the square will cheer,
Blow whistles, clap their hands.
Another year gone by,
A new one is quite near.

Each year the pages of the calendar
Float through the wintry air.
Memento pages,
Once tokens of remembrance,
Are only relics now.

Gone are the chronicles,
Gone, the old soggy files
Of yet another year gone by,
When many died in fratricidal wars,
Those worshipping the cross,
Those facing Mecca as they pray.

Gone are the printed images
Of infants, children, tots
With spindly legs, with spindly arms,
Their swollen bellies, vacant stares,
Born with a spark of hope, only to die
While groping for their mothers' breasts.

So let us cheer, let us hug, embrace,
As we, well fed, are standing in the square
Or on the ballroom dancing floor,
Gustily chanting the "Auld Lang Syne."
Is it to recall the year that fled?
Or do we cheer, in order to forget?

So let us raise the cup and drink,
Resolving once again to love and to sustain,
To forge the old sword into plowshares,
And into pruning hooks the spears,
As we resolve each year again,
Forgetting that at heart
We are purblind, amnesiac men.

The Enigma Road

The time is near, a decade, two at most,
A tenuous gift of one more year,
To walk the road ahead,
The endless road I trod so long,
The road from where I came,
The road we all must go.

The road an unknown hand had paved for us
When time began, a road without an end.
A road, the journey once began,
Leads to the same mysterious site
From which none has returned to tell.

We walk and walk.
Our footprints, deep or shallow,
Soon shall become obscured
By never-ceasing tides,
Burnished by the sand of time,
No sound, no echoes left.

It was a long and arduous trail,
A glimpse of sunlight
Here and there, a sweet embrace,
The giggle of a child at play,
A sweet whisper in the night,
A frown, a censure, an empty accolade.

Upon a time I walked through storm and gales
That blotted out the sun,
Through days of gloom and of despair,
When raindrops on my face
All had a salty taste
And all my words anathema.

A child, I ran with hurried steps,
To tag, or being tagged,
To chase, or being chased.
As a grown-up man, fatigued by toil,
In quarries or on a cobbler's bench,
I trotted tiredly and spent.

And on that lifelong endless trek,
I glimpsed at those I left behind
And those who passed and those ahead,
And those who tarried for a while,
And those I led to a canopy to wed,
And those I followed to their end and wept.

And now I walked the road all men must take,
And each time I raised my eyes
To read the signpost written in the sky,
One arrow there, none pointing back,
Another pointing way ahead,
"Enigma," each one said.

Perfection

How would I know
The perfect harmony of sound
Without a false note in a song's refrain,
Enjoy an apple's autumn blush
Without a wormhole or a stain?

A maiden's blush without a blemish
Is all too perfect to be real.
The perfect stillness of a forest night,
Save for the flutter of a frightened wing,
The footsteps of an animal in flight.

The turquoise velvet of a summer sky,
Without a leaden rainy day,
In time turns tedious to the eye,
The stillness of a pond
Without the rushing of a stream.

And so it is with my beloved.
How would I comprehend her soft caress,
Her kisses, and her smile
Without a sometime lament or a tear,
A silly spat once in a while?

My Rose

Come, come, bare-bottom child of mine,
Your spindly, thorny arms
Mere twigs stretched out to be embraced.
Disrobed, you're asking to be swaddled,
Kept warm, kept damp,
Your roots, myriad hungry mouths
To suckle the moist ground.

"Each morn, a thousand roses bring …"
Omar, the ancient poet, sang,
But humbly I ask
For you to be my only one,
At dawn to grace my garden bed,
White as the freshly fallen snow,
Or sanguine red.

Your petals pink, the edges red,
A maiden's courtship blush,
You stretch your limbs
To greet the summer sky.
For every rose there is a painful thorn,
The sages claim, but I deny.
To me your scent atones for being stung.

Weep not. At season's end
You too must fade,
As we must all in time,
But until then bestow your charm,
Your hues, your sweet incense,
Sweet maiden of my garden realm.

My Valentine

It's cold, the sky,
A panhandler's, pauper's,
Windswept and forlorn,
Wanting and lost.

And then soft sounds reach my ear—
A murmur, a faint melody,
An old refrain I hear,
The pain has gone; my heart can beat again.

I recognize it now,
For it was you, my love.
You never left.
You always stood there at my side.
My vision dimmed for only a short while.

Unseen you were,
Unseen yet there,
To touch with an unseen heart.
Spouse, comrade, wife—
Take any other name you want—
To me, you are my life.

The End Was Near

Suddenly the clock struck hard,
Vanished, gone the dulcet chime,
Dividing night from day,
The throbbing clock to herald once again
The morning glow.

The chime struck hard,
And in that deadly knell
My vision dimmed,
And suddenly a gloomy dusk
Eclipsed the midday sun
And day gave way to night.

The wheels of time began to slow,
The gears no longer meshed.
They slowed but didn't cease to turn.
They mustn't stop, not yet, not yet,
Moving my lips, I whispered to myself.

I couldn't see but knew
That all the rivers ceased to flow.
The roads ahead of me
Had reached their end.
Here stood the sign: "Nothing Beyond."

Not yet, not yet, I wished to say
With a pain-constricted throat
And mutely moved my lips,
A beggar begging for another day,
A grant, an offering, a gift.

Then stillness all around me,
Cold, chilling,
Bleak, solemn,
An utter silence only I could hear.

A spark lit somewhere,
A soft whisper far away,
The fluttering of lips
Of other men, not mine,
Staring at the glassy screen with knitted brows.

And from my ebbing pain,
I rose to greet another day,
And the stillness of the night
Gave rise to a soft tune
Of rippling waves.
The river flowed again.

They spoke, the men in scrub suit blue,
A whisper, hushed, an undertone,
"Look, look, it beats again, his heart,
A rhythm, and extra beat, a sigh."
Their solemn chat rings in my empty ears.
They spoke of life, not death.

And still unsure whose life was on the scale,
Light flooded the darkened stage.
The pain abated and I perceived
That life grew wings.
It was my life, the whisperer's refrain.

It was my life and I was home again.
The thistles in my heart
Gave way to lips,
Soft, roseate upon my sweaty brow,
For she was there beside me—
Her seal, her affirmation, and her vow.

Memories

I can no longer recollect the names
Of towns, those of my many friends,
The labor in the quarries on scorching summer days,
The numbing chill, my frozen hands, the icy rails,
The gnawing hunger, the jailer's lash, the many ills.

My memory, a coarse-meshed sieve
Of many days gone by,
The hate, the curses, maledictions,
The coarse, striped cloth, the misty rain,
An emblem on my chest,
A number for my name.

Gone are the many women, men,
The good, the evil ones,
The many who I cherished once,
The fragrance of a lilac sprig,
Or was it just the soft caress,
A loving woman's hand?

There is one day beyond erase,
A day, an ancient obelisk
Impervious to the ravages of times,
The way we stood there,
Thousands with bundles at our feet.

But to my eyes she was the only one,
A child, a daughter, a mother,
Clutching hands,
Mine clutching hers convulsively,
She gently pushing me away.

With downcast gaze,
A stifled whisper,
An echo of a sob, she was telling me
The time had come for us to part,
To part, perhaps to never meet again.

That I, her son,
Her only child, must run
While there was time
Before the gate was closed beyond recall,
But she, bound by a filial duty of her own,
She could not go, she must remain.

I still recall her trembling hand,
Our downcast eyes to hide our tears.
If clasping hands could speak
And racing hearts could scream,
These were the loudest farewells.
None can erase that day.

Tattoos

We bear tattoos on our arms,
So many more in our hearts,
Blue inked, indelible, beyond erase,
For all to see, a sore to our tired eyes.

We've learned to grieve in silence,
Bear our wounds with consternation.
And when we speak, be it in prose or verse,
We hide them from the fickle light of day,
From comments, innuendos, callousness, ill will.

And though we hope and wish
For our wounds to heal,
And like the sky at dusk
Their blue to fade, each number
Takes to wings and flees unseen
And yet tenaciously they cling, they stay.

And while we hope
That they will fade,
A healing hand with time
Erases our wishes, our fervent pleas,
Silently flow the sifting sands,
The hourglass becoming emptier each day.

Longing

The greeter of the rising sun,
I watch the end of days,
And with a tired eye and wrinkled brow,
I gaze upon the setting sun.

I follow its descent with aching heart
And wish the pendulum of time would slow
To halt, perchance to cease its stride
For one more while.

Return, bring back, I wish,
The tingling of the skin,
The swiftness of my legs
That longed to run.

To run nowhere,
No place, only to run
To hear the wind
Commingle with the panting of my breath.

To let my legs grow wings again
And flap my arms in flight,
To fly, to soar nowhere,
No longer earthbound, just to fly.

To let my timeworn eyes
See once again and gaze
Upon a sea, azure, a hidden dell,
A cloud, a rushing brook, a bridal veil.

To hear again, clear and unfettered
Words, sweetly uttered rhymes,
Melodious songs of mockingbirds,
The murmur of the rippling tide.

To smell the fragrance
Of a daisy, a dew-clad blade of grass,
The rose along my picket fence,
The iridescent blue of thistle, vying with the sky.

To embrace, caress, to kiss young lips,
To whisper words invented on the go,
To be foolish, to be asinine
And heedless once again.

The Conch

I found a conch upon the shore,
Half-buried in the sand,
Pink, salt-crusted, pitted,
Buffeted, tossed by the ebb
And by the flowing tide,
Gently swaying to and fro,
Bidding me to pick it up,
To set it free, to let it go.

I placed it to my ear
And listened to its whisper.
"Come to the sea, far, far away,
Where no one dared to venture yet,"
It spoke to me
In singsong of the sand and sea.

"Come where the windswept, sparkling waves
Mirror the sun in multicolored hues,
Pellucid, sky-hued, emerald at noon.
At night the lustrous moon
Spreads silver on the surf,
And all is calm and all serene.

Sanguine though and dark at times,
The sea thunders angrily; it roars
At the buffeting and leaden sky,
Heaving, whirling, white-crested,
A dancing dervish, a drunken tar.

Playful and tumbling at other times,
A puppy dog, a newborn colt,
A child in the meadows at springtime,
Dancing, twisting, a young lion
Tossing his mane, pawing at the sky.

But down below the water's skin,
Life throbs in its deep-bosomed realm,
Life, agreeable, plankton-laden,
Primordial life, the womb of all that is alive today,
The cradle of all things on foot or in the air,
Even of you, you curious man.

Deep down, unseen to you,
The smiling dolphins play,
And shoals of silver fish
Like ballerinas dance,
The stingrays flap their angel wings,
The crawling starfish,
Stars fallen from the sky.

Are you still listening, old man?
Just nod your head.
I've told my tale so many times,
The designated spokesman of the sea.
I am verbose, long-winded;
I ramble on and on
Like an aged actor, like an old ham.

I feel the trembling of your hand
And sense the frowning of your brow.
What is the glamour of the sea? you ask,
Half-spoken like a man.
You shake your head.
I do detect a smirk upon your face.

What is the virtue living there? you wish to know.
You upright-walking, bipedal man
Who built the pyramids,
Exploded atom bombs,
Flew faster than the speed of sound,
Claimed to be master of us all.

Well, let me whisper it to you
In my conch idiom of the sea.
There is no bondage there, no slavery.
There are no killing fields, no Holocaust,
For man has never lived beneath the waves

And so you see, old man,
Down at the bottom of the sea,
The graveyard of your detritus,
Your ships, a sailor's last ahoy,
The many plundered treasure troves,
And yet, in spite of it, all this
Is freedom land, my dear."

Deliverance

We are free now,
Unfettered and unshackled,
Free as the wind,
Capriciously unbound
To tilt the sails,
To turn the windmill wings.

Free as the swallows
To choose the eaves,
To build their nests in spring,
The warbler picks its branch
To sing amid the leaves.

We are free now,
Though we dare not look behind,
For each one casts
A shadow of his past,
The remnants of his yoke
Of whom he was.

Of Things Ephemeral

The miracles of life,
Walt Whitman's *Leaves of Grass*,
The mockingbird, its song,
The apes to Jane Goodall,
To us, our God,
To God, the universe at large.

The newborn child,
Blessed in its innocence,
The toothless smile, the grasping hand,
The cooing in its crib, its song,
Its first poetic utterances at dawn.

The crystal spring that gushes from a rock,
Earth's gift to quench the thirsty man,
The spider clinging to the moss,
The emperor penguin, the egg between his toes,
Braving the arctic storm.

The eager groom, the blushing bride,
The sigh, the language of the night,
The sound, the touch,
The spark, a lightning bolt,
Invisibly begetting man.

To soothe his ignorance, his fears,
Combating monsters in his sleep—
Man coined it miracle of life.
Is it a miracle indeed,
Or is it only make-believe?

Abstractions, concepts, esoteric laws,
The endlessness of space, of time,
Eternity, without beginning, without end,
A sham they are, a self-deceptive lie.
For eons hence the end will come
By stealth, by frost, by fire from the sky.

The flaming star above will burst,
The earth, a barren comet aimlessly adrift,
And man-made God, that sallow-bearded man
With so much sorrow in his face,
With death of man, God too will die.

The Echo of the Past

Beyond the seven mountains and the seven seas,
Beyond Sambation, the Rubicon, and Styx,
The sounds of my life had come to a halt,
The terminus, the final stop, the end
Of my allotted time between then and now.

Here stands the sentinel,
Winged brother to the man at Eden's gate.
"No trespassing," says the flaming sign,
But if you wish to hear
Your life resound again,
Turn back. The echoes of your past
Are in the shadows and quite near.

And like the albatross around your neck,
Your past is there, unseen to none but you,
The past all men must learn to bear.
It is their deadweight,
A refuge or a blessing,
To some a sad anathema.

"Beware the past," the winged man spoke,
"For in your retrospective journey there
Are other gates, inviting some.
They lead to paradise.
Some lead to hell,
Most to the quicksand of your mind."

I turn at my shadow and nod consent
At my companions of the past,
And hear the muted ticking of a clock.
The sounds I thought had ceased
Obediently came back,
Scraping and bowing,
Elbowing each other,
Anxious to be first.

I hear an infant cry,
His mother's first,
The rustling of a shirt,
The softness of the breast, a lullaby,
A couplet with the infant's cooing.
"I wed thee"—words upon a time,
Now only shards.

A murky study room,
A splintered wooden bench,
The teacher dozing off, asleep,
And I, the student, diffident, averse,
Recite unwillingly in half-song
Black dots, the alphabet of long ago.

And then I sing
The circle, round and round,
Feet stomping on the dusty floor,
Thanking the Lord for the sun, the sky,
The restless feet allowed to chase
A yellow butterfly,
To run with a dog, to kick a soggy ball.

Striped men and sunken eyes,
A bowl in hand, we stand in line,
Stooped backs and shuffling feet.
And walking to the fence
I see a friend of mine
About to touch the wire strands.
No, no. I turn my face. No longer can I gaze,
Too long my shadow, too much, too much.
I wish my shadow farewell, good-bye.

The River

Light-footed, half-carried aloft by the wind,
I ran along the trodden path,
My running mate, the river down below,
Only a brook, but to my eye
A mighty river then.

The melting snow, the springtime rains,
My river tumbles, ocher, muddy,
Whipped by a gauntlet of overhanging boughs.
Full of anger, it roars.
Rushing, it spills its banks
To reach the tranquil comfort of the sea.

Craving for the past,
I have returned to visit my old friend,
My former running mate.
I was a boy then;
Now I am a stooped old man,
Resting my arms on the bridge's wooden rail.

I gaze with longing eye
At what was once my river down below,
A muddy brook, a rivulet, a trickle now—
Oil-sleeked, weed-overgrown, the current slow.
With hesitating steps I reach the edge.
Gone are the pollywogs, the croaking toads.
Only a stillness now remains.

Was there a river many years ago,
The barking of a mongrel dog,
The milkman's wagon clattering
Along the cobbled street at dawn,
A bearded man in gabardine,
Walking, a cane to pace his gait?

Was ever there a boy with racing feet,
Daring the river of his youth, daring the wind,
Or is it just an old man's dream,
A silent dirge for things that were
And now forever gone?

The Blue Jay

Come, blue jay, do not fear.
Come closer, as you come each day
To shake your crested head at me,
Your song a rattling of an empty can,
You beggar screeching for some alms.
And with distrust you then procure,
And without thanks you dart away.

With feathers for a diadem,
The way you strut
Along my humble windowsill,
The way you always preen,
The way you screech,
You certainly must be an avian queen.

I do not know your name,
You stranger on the piney bough,
Nor do you know who I might be.
It doesn't matter, beggar friend,
We know each other just the same.
You are a bird, I am a man;
The bread crumbs are for you to claim.

To Remember Them

We are the fallen leaves,
The mold, the detritus of life,
Discarded, youth never to return,
And yet we still are there
In dog-eared sepia photographs,
Remembered in a song.

We are the stooped beneath the peddler's bag,
Shopkeepers standing on the threshold of his store
And murmuring with sullen stares,
An invitation to come in to buy
Or just to look at our wares.

The men behind the butcher's block,
The pushcart men, their pleading voice,
The cobblers, smithies, handymen,
Once architects of pyramids, now only of adobe huts,
Beating the cadences of our toil with quill and pen.

Slaves once, then masters, and then slaves again,
The makers of a rich men's furs,
And diadems to crown the kings
And for the poor
The patches on their pants.

Although our backs are bent,
And our beards are gray,
We still discuss, debate,
And circumnavigate
The words of our sage,
The wisdom of the yesterdays.

Though you've watched and wept,
Seeing us squatting in a marketplace
And then boarding trains, never to be seen again,
Was it only an illusion,
A sleight of hand of the Almighty,
Or a bad dream?

As long as we recall
The cobblestones on which we trod,
The musty odor of the narrow lanes,
And while we still can hear the plaintive songs
Of swaying, bearded men,
Beseeching on a Sabbath day,
We will remember them.

The Morning Mist

The fog lifts
At dawn,
A fisherman's net,
Drenched and waterlogged,
Drawn by the cold and stubby fingers
Of men tending the sea.

A milky coat
Sprayed on my windowpanes.
Far off, I hear the singing
Of a mockingbird,
The tuning of a fiddle,
Before the melody begins.

The foghorn's plaintive song,
Only a lilting mantra hum,
Doors slam, dogs bark,
The garbage can a brassy drum,
A jogger's slapping footsteps.

New tunes are there
To wake the day,
The men behind the wheels
Revving their cars,
A euphony to modern ears,
Shattering the mystery of night.

The dawn cast off the morning veil,
A spray of sun has lit the poplar trees,
Soft-swaying candles
On the altar of another day,
The hills dark painted until now,
No longer ashen gray,
Are now aglow.

I've cast my dreams aside.
Dew-scented light
Erased my nightly apparitions.
The mist of night
Has given way to day.
The clock has chimed again.

Look Up

Look up, my children,
Look, the stars are there,
Erased each day
By solar light,
A sponge against
The azure tablet
To tell us day
From night.

Look up, my children,
The stars are there,
As yet unseen
But have no fear,
The sun will set,
The clouds will part,
The fog will clear,
And you will
See them once again.

Look up and see
A broken necklace string,
And a million pearls strewn
Upon the canopy of night—
No broom to sweep them up
No hands to gather them,
To string them once again.

Look, can you see
The great Orion,
The Northern Polar star,
The Milky Way,
The blushing planet Mars,
The faithful guardians
Of the men at sea?
They twinkle with a lullaby
For us to dream.

Remember

Look down upon the ground,
You *Herrenvolk*, and shed a tear.
The footprints of your past are there,
Embedded in eternal stone,
Etched into the skin of the earth,
Cut with a whip into the solid crust,
The never-healing welts upon the backs
Of those you have enslaved.

Look there, the imprints
Of the many walking men,
Millions of feet, some large,
Some small, a child, a woman,
The young, the lame, the very old,
Reluctant children dragging tired feet.

And over there a tattered shoe,
A wooden clog, a prison cap,
An imprint of a hand
Of those who begged
To be allowed to live another day,
While trudging to an unmarked grave.

Look at those footprints
Up and down your roads.
They are the wormholes of your land,
Of you who gazed at the heavens
In search of long-forgotten Gods
And bleated like so many sheep,
Ein Volk, ein Reich, ein Fuehrer,
Look now and weep.

The Empty Street

They've gone, save for a slinking cat,
A sparrow searching for a grain,
A leaf aflutter in the breeze,
Shards from a shattered windowpane,
An empty pram,
Leaning with one wheel
Down in the curbside gutter.

The empty huts, the thatch,
Eaves like straw visors
Against the scorching summer heat,
Smashed window, doors ajar,
The sunken eyes of blinded men
In search of light of yesterday.

They walked those twisting alleys,
The back streets, the rutted lanes,
Somber-faced men and women,
Children clutching to their skirts,
The swaddled infants in their arms.

Then came a time of mercy,
A time of accidents—or was it luck?—
When I could walk those streets again,
Empty, parched, and barren,
The crooked, sun-bleached pavement stones,
Crushed riverbeds, empty of men,
Desolate and silent.

Ill at ease, my steps resounded
Like hollow drumbeats,
Echoes of once distant volleys
Still pounding in my ears.
My heart, a caged bird,
With clipped, imprisoned wings,
Beat frantically against my ribs,
The ghetto fence.

They're gone, save for a slinking cat,
A sparrow searching for a grain,
A windswept leaf aflutter in the breeze,
Shards from a shattered windowpane,
An empty pram,
Leaning with one wheel
Down in the curbside gutter.

The empty huts, the thatch,
Eaves like straw visors
Against the scorching summer heat,
Smashed windowpanes
Like sunken eyes of blinded men
In search of light of yesterday.

They've gone, never to return,
Taken away, the children in midsong,
The jump rope coiled,
The empty pram,
An open book with dog-eared leaves,
Only the wind to turn the page.

And awed I stood and wondered,
Was it a phantom, an apparition?
Was it reality, a haunting dream?
And in my darkest night of nights
I saw them walking ceaselessly,
The very old, the young, the spry,
Unwanted by their fellow men,
They walked, for they must die.

Am I alive?
Am I obliged, compelled
With every heavy-lidded dusk
Etched in my dreams,
To die with them
And every dawn to live again,
To live and to remember?

The Garden of Eden

Come, you sons of Abraham,
Cease longing for the lands you've left.
It was no earthly paradise;
It was an earthly hell.

Polluted, weed-infested land of bitter fruits,
Where even roses had a putrid smell,
And the inhabitants,
Blond, blue-eyed serpents,
Your pugilistic friends.

You were expelled for daring to partake
Of wisdom and of lore.
You have transgressed
Beyond redemption.
You've sinned beyond amends.

And in that other paradise,
You and your branded sons
Were shown the exit gate,
As you've been shown since then,
Unwelcome you were there
And everywhere you went
Since the dawn of men.

Wilted now, the gardens of your Babylon,
Jerusalem, a vale of tears,
Saintly kings, wise prophets,
Men of prose and song,
Of parchments and of scrolls,
The temples, scattered stones,
Lay ruined at your feet.

The dulcet notes of your Espania,
Discordant music to your ears,
Flames, chanting hooded monks,
The ringing bells that tolled
Of holiness and death
Under the shadow of the cross.

Once venerated Schiller, Goethe, Kant—
Their pugilistic sons exchanged
The quills for hobnailed boots and guns,
No longer *Liebeslieder*,
No longer dulcet tunes, cantatas, chants,
Their songs a chilling hymn to death.

And you, the worshippers of one and only God,
The chosen ones, the shining light
That blinded other men
And branded you the outcasts of their realms,
Are you still craving for the past?
Must you be shown the door again?

The Flight

Run, run, my kinsman.
Run, do not turn to gaze,
And do not grieve
With teary eye
Over the conflagration of your life.

Do not look back.
Run, run in haste.
Nostalgia for the past
Is nothing but a waste
To sap your strength.

You're not the first.
How many times from distant shores
Your father and their fathers fled,
Their voices muted echoes now,
Their tears, sap of their wounded souls.

Reaching the sea, tumbled by the sand,
Tears turned to amber,
Each one another bead
In the long necklace of your past,
Another exile to recall.

A Reminder

I write, my hand,
My letters reel from side to side,
A drunkard's midnight stride.

And yet I write,
Compelled to speak,
To break the silence
Of a heartache night.

So let the written word
Become a sleight of hand,
An act of magic
To conjure up the past.

No arias there,
A simple melody,
A mumbled song,
A wordless hum.

Each phrase a signpost,
A reminder who I was
Not long ago,
And who I am,
Or think I am, today.

Free at Last

Free at last, like the blushing leaf,
Free to spread my wings and soar,
The autumn-gilded butterfly
Carried aloft by the updrafts of the air,
No longer do I need to flap my wings.

I'm free to wade through mounds
Of fallen autumn leaves
And listen to the whispers
Of wind-stirred branches,
My full orchestral score.

My pebbly garden path to walk along,
The Eden of my waning years,
Hands in my pockets,
Merrily tapping my foot
In rhyme to a warbler's song.

Unshackled, freed from days
Of wooden clogs and prison garb,
I praise the sky, the golden hills,
The lichen-painted stones,
The music of a nearby child at play.

I must no longer scrape
Or bow, or bend my aching back
To please. No longer must I weep.
No longer do I thirst
Nor yearn for food.

I'm free at last and do not care
If others frown at all my sins,
No longer placate idols of the past.
Gone is the awe, the heedless worship
Of my capricious Gods.

At last I bask in full recollection
The many moments of the past.
I'm the never-sated hummingbird,
Though tired are my wings.
The sunset near, I'm satisfied at last.

The Mist on the Hill

Reluctantly, the shrouding mist
Lifts, drawn by numb fingers,
A fisherman, his tangled net,
On a gray and chilly dawn.

The red-tailed hawk is on the wing
To ride the up-drift of the air.
The foghorns on the bay,
Base fiddlers of the night,
No longer moan their plaintive cries.

The dusky hills are lit again;
I fix my gaze upon them
With drowsy, morning eyes.
My limbs astir again,
I bid adieu the night.

The misty curtain's lacy hem
Has reached the dusky sky.
A eucalyptus tree along the crest
Began its morning sway
To greet the sun, its morning guest.

The climbing sun
Has set aflame the wind-caressed
And sun-bleached oats,
The Scotch broom, yellow mustard.
Gnarled clumps of oaks
Have cast their shadows on the ground.

I've come to greet the light,
One man's call to joy,
Remembering the days
When darkness fell upon my eyes,
And unlike then, I gaze and smile.

Two does, Aurora's children
Enter from the misty shade
To greet another day,
A day for them—
The day is also mine.

The Garden in May

My bride, the month of May,
My canopy, the branches of my apple tree—
I am the groom.
It is my garden's wedding day.

No winter chill, no frost,
But petal snowflakes—
A shower of confetti
Lands on my nuptial garb,
My garden apparel, my jaunty hat.

Daylilies, Irish bluebells,
The wedding flowers at my feet,
The revelers, the nectar-drinking,
Base-fiddling bumblebees
Reeling from cup to flower cup,
Already drunk in ecstasy.

The blue jays are my wedding guests.
The larks, pedestrian sparrows,
The merry-making mockingbirds,
My music makers for the day,
Are here to serenade.

And in their song I hear
The preacher's wedding words:
"To everything there is a season,
There is a time to plant, a time to reap.
A time to bloom, a time to fruit."

"Let it be," I hear a whisper in the wind.
"Let it be," nods the bud-heavy bough.
The sun has reached the hidden crest,
Setting my revelers aglow,
And as I listen with enchanted ear,
I sing along, "Oh, yes, so let it be,
So let it be, my dear."

Dreams

Defiant of the sandman's rule,
Some never dream,
But I, attuned to the flutter
Of a night owl's wing,
Am lulled to sleep
And, having fled reality, embrace pretense.
Dissolve the real me.

When dusk becomes the gate to dream,
I vanish from myself,
Plunge into a nonexistent realm
Where only darkness looms
Without beginning, without end.
When time is shown the door,
The clock turns mute.
The pendulum has ceased to swing.

And in that flight of fantasy,
Self-exiled, being all alone,
Concealed from man-made storms,
And from abysmal ruin,
I find repose and solitude,
A place where man-made storms
No longer rage.

I am afraid to tell my dreams,
A travesty, a mockery,
Anathema to some,
A discord minor sound,
A dissonance to many ears.

A stream of light, my wake-up call,
I hear the ticking of a clock,
And know it was a lie, a fanciful illusion,
The quenching of a thirst, a moment's flight.
I am alive to greet the day.
The next-door children sing again.

Home, Sweet Home

My native land, my home,
How well I do recall
That land of mine,
A land, of nocturnes,
mazurkas, polonaise.

The land of
Hills, marshes, sandy shores,
The cold and windy Baltic Sea,
And long-abandoned castles on its hills,
Hooded monks and black-robed priests,
The strutting officers in shining boots.

The black Madonna on the hill,
White roses clutching to her heart,
The gilded altars lit by candlelight,
Hands folded, breviaries, and rosaries,
Black shawls, bent heads,
Kneeling in prayer, mumbling men.

There stood the old adobe hut,
The fading whitewashed paint,
The thatch, rain barrels under eaves,
The ever-present mold, the soot,
A dingy room, the earthen floor.
Here I was born; here my cradle stood.

Back alleys, rutted paths,
The heat of summer dust, the autumn mud,
The wintry flurries, the frozen pond,
My father's shouts in anger, some in jest,
His songs, his speech, my lullabies—
This was my shelter; this was my nest.

I was a barefoot boy, daring the wind,
Kicking the boy-made dust,
The roadside ditch, a brook, a little stream,
The stinging nettle weeds,
The shadow of my apple tree,
A place to dream.

A rooster's heralding the dawn,
My morning wake-up call,
A summon to another day,
The schoolboy walking with his shuffling feet,
A dingy room, a splintered wooden bench,
And singsong recitation of an ancient text.

Midsummer light, black shadows in the dust,
The heat of day, the chill at night,
The mud-streaked banks of melting snow,
The icicles upon the eaves,
The flight of bats across the purple sky,
The naked trees, another year gone by.

My land of sun-bleached barns,
Familiar faces, forgotten now,
Though some I still recall—
Gaunt, weather-beaten, and begrimed,
The young, the old, the haggard,
Those full of hope, those long resigned.

Once they were there, the bearded old,
The young grown old before their time,
Yakovs, Yossefs, Solomons,
The pushcart peddlers, traders,
Toilers toting bundles on their backs,
So many stooped beneath
The burden of their lives.

They've gone; they are no more,
But I, with bow upon my cello's strings,
Hear the Klezmer flute, base fiddle, drums,
The sound of dancing feet,
And on a Sabbath afternoon I hear them sing.
I see them nod and sway.
Bereaved I wish they were still there.

The Gift

If death be not the end,
When time has no more meaning
And all my thoughts have lost their sound,
Then I shall gift my flesh to fragrant dust,
In neither joy nor sorrow.

And on that day when I must die,
Death not an end but a new beginning,
A whispered word, an agonizing cry,
Then I shall miss a soft caressing hand,
A children's blissful song, an infant's smile,
An old familiar face.

To eternity let me bestow my memories,
The beauty of a new awakened sky,
On a sweet-scented April day,
The swaying of a poplar in the wind,
The bursting buds of a cherry tree
The fragrance of a rose,
The rippling of the brook.

Gladly shall I bring these
To the place where all our souls
Are said to drift,
And place them there,
A gift in gratitude of having lived.

The Mystery of Time

Speak to me, dear physicist,
Of particles that swirl with speed of light,
Of apogees, trajectories,
Those that you so cleverly scan,
Who fashioned them, the protons, electrons,
And placed them all alight.

Who pushed the cosmic pendulum to swing,
Placed numbers on the face of clocks,
Then fashioned men, enchanted by their ring,
Men who would name the flow of time,
Men who could fly, could walk, could swim?

Who created earth's gravity
For men to walk, for butterflies to fly,
The blossoms on a branch each spring,
The water rushing down a brook,
The doves and falcons on the wing?

Who set the moon to spin around the earth,
To be for us the lunar date, the monthly score,
The hand that hurled the earth to spin
Around the sun, then set ablaze its core?

Who struck the first percussion wave
Against the drum of our curious human ears,
For us to hear and to perceive the sound,
The rods, the cones, the lens in our eyes?

Unfold those mysteries of time, dear physics man.
Who created infinity of space and why?
Who cast the light upon the sea
So we may fathom when it all began
And when the end might come?

156

Old Man Levko

Old Levko was his name, a tiller of the soil,
Clasping the handles of his plow,
Gnarled fingers, weather-beaten face,
The gleaming blade, the prow,
Cleaving the earthen waves,
Churning a stubble-covered row.

Whoa! I still can hear his shout,
The swishing of his whip
Upon the straining nag, its hollow back,
The yoke, the bit, the foamy sweat,
Black ravens swooping down
To feast upon the upturned row.

In times of plenty, of abundant crests of golden wheat,
Old Levko was content. He was the sovereign
Over his land, his hut, his children, and his wife,
But there were other days, stark famine days
Of barren fields, of stunted sheaves, of hungry eyes.
An evil eye had struck, and Levko cursed.

And so he labored on his land,
With plow and harrow, sickle, and his scythe,
The soil, his flesh, his blood,
Stooped, bent—I see him now,
Shielding his eyes against the glaring sky,
Wiping his face, his tired brow.

Well, I recall the squeaking wheel,
The water splashing back into the well,
The village church, the Sunday morning bell,
The gilded dome, the double-transom cross,
The scented air, the pew,
The singing of a hymn.

Empty the church, the villagers have left,
Their prayers ceased,
The bearded priest, the acolytes have gone,
Old Levko in his pew, the only one,
No longer can he hear, no longer see,
And none to recall his name.

The Winds of Time

Be kind, be gentle, eternal winds of time.
Let the few maple leaves still flutter on the bough
Before they turn to autumn brown,
And, seeking shelter on the ground,
Become the wintry eiderdown.

Be gentle with the shuffling man,
Round-shouldered, weighted down
By burdens long beyond recall,
Once keeper of the gate and now unknown.
Be gentle in his autumn years.

And let him dream a while.
Give him your gifts, your alms.
To him whose past
And present have become but one,
Be gentle with the shuffling man.

Dreamers

Your dreams, your playmates of the night,
Descend upon you
In silent shoes like thieves,
The moonlight casting silver halos
On softly swaying drapes.

I see a smile across your musing lips.
Sleep well, my mate, the sandman sings
Your nightly lullaby.
You nod your head, you sigh,
The curtains softly sway.

At times, my dreams
Do enter with a thud,
A herd of horses at full gallop
With thunder, foam-lipped, all unshod,
While grim-faced riders urge them on.

An avalanche of shouts,
Of languages I once have known,
Pale, misty phantoms,
Enigmas, mystifying, a cracked mirror,
A forgery, a mockery of who I am,
Or who someday I might become.

Late Autumn Days

Long past the harvest days,
The wintry cold
Comes creeping in by stealth.
The morning dew turns into rime
And hoarfrost blankets,
The brown-spotted stubble
Of past summer rye.

Long before the hush of night,
His trembling hand
Clutches the old gnarled cane,
Once his companion,
Waiting to be used again,
The cane his father braced
In his own autumn time.

Silent the hut now,
Silent the treadle, the spinning wheel,
The mournful, plaintive songs—
No infant squall, no sullen discontent,
His sons, one gone to war, never to return,
A scoffer, Antichrist the other,
A daughter, errant and forlorn.

He leaves the hut, the bearer of the cane,
Tall once, no longer need to bend,
Beneath the lintel of the door,
The rusty hinges, the timeworn stoop,
The whitewashed crumbling walls.

Wearily he walks, the stooped old man,
For out there bids the leaf-strewn path,
Softly to cushion his stride.
The yellow leaves too had come to rest,
Their summer days unspent.

He walks with swaying stride,
The night, the season of the parting,
Between the being and the dream,
Stark and eternal,
Awaits the night without a dawn,
And there ahead, in still anticipation,
A bench hewn from a log.

Shaped by his father,
It stands beneath the tree
At the pond's edge,
A place to rest, to dream,
Like many others who came here,
Summoned by the night without a day.

I Only See Myself

How often have I walked
The cobbled streets,
The crumbling, littered sidewalks,
Stepped over putrid gutters,
My eyes upon my weary feet,
But rarely saw many
Squat against the crumbling walls,
Their hungry eyes, the wistful gaze,
The sunken cheeks.
Though I caught sight of them,
I only saw myself.

And in the days of famine,
How often have I walked
The twisting country lanes,
Along a split rail, weather-beaten fence,
The barren fields,
The rusty, long-abandoned plows,
The gaunt and raw-boned nags,
The stubble-searching cows,
The many stooped with hoe in hand,
But only saw myself.

In terror-stricken days,
I ran to save my life.
Fear-stricken and with pounding heart,
I ran, oblivious to so many others
In our headless flight
And overcome by horror
And by a paralyzing fright.
I only saw myself.

And later on, while searching for a better land,
The wings of peace my sails,
Horizons still far off,
I and my shipmates
Gazed upon the parting waves.
We gazed and dreamed,
And even then
I only sought salvation of myself.

And even now,
About to ebb their flow,
With failing sight and muted sound,
I gaze upon the mirror of the past,
Abashed by what had been.
I try to see what lies ahead,
Beyond the curtain of the known,
And still, I only see myself.

A Plea to Erato

If I could use only my words,
Each one a scented petal of a rose,
Mellifluous and without barbs,
Devoid of wilt and slow decay.

Words to console, not vilify,
Poignant, without prattle,
To be whispered, not shouted,
Lilting words, not harsh,
Conveying passion.

Words flowing, rushing,
Like a mountain spring,
Each one a sonnet,
"Scheherazade," recite and sing
To calm her sultan's ire.

Teach me to use a simple phrase,
Iambic pentameters,
Or plain blank verse,
A limerick, a nurse's rhyme,
My pen a master's brush
To soothe the weary eye.

Now in the season of denuded boughs
And wilting leaves of yesterday,
So much already has been lost
In sorrow and dismay.
Let me not lose my words;
Just let them be mine and stay.

Silence

Hush now, let silence reign
Along the empty streets,
Where children hopped and skipped,
And lovers, arms entwined,
Went on their sunset stroll,
And bearded men walked on and on.

Hush now, let silence reign
Over an old man's chant,
The laughter of a child,
A mother's frantic call.

Hush now, the silent homes,
The windows with their broken panes
Stare soullessly like blinded men,
Each home, each hut a solemn tomb.

Only a brooding echo
Within the rooms of broken doors,
Of unmade beds, of empty cribs,
Of silent clocks upon the walls.

Hush now, the silence of a town,
Not of repose, it is the silence of demise,
Of broken songs,
Each one a dirge of things now gone.

Gone is the songstress of a lullaby.
Gone are the children in her arms.
Gone are the medleys, the last children's cry,
Gone, never to return.

Silently I beg, no more, never again,
The sound of hobnailed boots,
The rumbling of a distant train,
The clanking of a gun, the rattling of a chain.

Hush now, my fellow man,
Let tearful silence reign.

The Homeless

I see you, fellow homeless man,
Squatting on the sidewalk.
Wordlessly you beg with bloodshot eyes.
Is it a piece of bread you crave?
Is it the balm to soothe your pain?

You squat, you stand with unkempt beard,
Unwashed and clad in tattered pants,
The ever-present cardboard sign your calling card,
Clasped in your weather-beaten hands.

I know you well,
For once upon a time,
I too used doorways, stoops, a soggy bench.
Like you, I sought a glance, an affirmation
That I was man, like other men.

And sheltered for the many days,
And sheltered for the many nights,
Cold shelters were my realm,
My vision, my horizons,
Rows upon rows of man-made thorns.

I dare not meet your gaze,
For once, bereft of home,
I also knew compassion's stingy hand.
Because of faith or color of our skin,
We were despised by fellow men.

Today I walk along the well-paved streets,
Halt at the many crosswalk lights,
My springy steps, my patent shoes,
Soft leather gloves,
Well groomed and satisfied.

I swerve; I shun your gaze.
It is a wound that never healed,
And giving haste to my quick stride,
I dare not run, and yet I wish
To be far from where I've come.

With eyes averted
And with trembling hand,
I reach for a coin—no, not a coin,
Only a token for a wishful breach
Between my past and now.

Farewell to My Prison Clogs

Let me embrace you one more time,
As you embraced my blistered heels,
My soles, half-frozen toes,
On days of ice,
On days of summer scorch.

Nocturnal mates of weary rest,
Forced marches, tramping in a prison yard,
The pillows for my tired head,
And dreams of open skies and fragrant moss.

You had been there to soothe my head
When searchlight-splintered starlit skies;
A sandman moon hung limply
Between the wire strands.

Each day we marched to toil
The deathly quarry, the sandy, rocky ground.
Clip-clop you sang along with other clogs,
A prisoner's beating heart, our song.

Farewell, my clogs, sabots, clodhoppers,
The Sabbath of the toil arrived at last.
Your splintered soles, the worn-down heels,
Ask for a respite, as does my heart, as does my soul.

Rest in the attic of my unwanted dreams,
And gather dust, the dust of peace.
Go rest and let us hope no man to ever wear
The prison clogs or hobnailed boots.

Some claim that we may meet again,
Old comrade of so many years ago,
And in that realm of dust to dust,
My dust and yours be one.

A Love Poem

Two scores and ten,
I drew your face with trembling hand
Upon a canvas of my mind,
My signature, an oath,
A ring, a wedding band.

Each day I look upon it,
It is still there,
The wistful gaze,
The same soft eyes—
They haven't changed.

Your voice, more mellow to my ear
And yet I crave to hear
The songs you sang so softly
A day ago, a week, a year,
In days of pain, in days of joy.

The canvas drawn upon,
A precious mirror now
Of every day, and every night
I look at it and see you there,
At dusk, at dawn, my shining light.

I Can Hear

Lulled by encroaching silence
Of a lifelong span of time,
I still can hear the sweet harmony
Of pebbles gliding in the tide,
Their E-flat pebble song
In contrapuntal ripple of the waves.

I can hear the children sing
"Humpty Dumpty,"
"Ring Around the Rosie,"
The cries, the laughter,
The chiming of their little bells,
The atonality of their songs.

I can hear the brassy drone
Of black-winged bumblebees,
Base fiddle player's monophonic hum,
And those aloft, the mockingbirds,
The mimes, the mimics,
The thieves of avian songs.

The polyphonic rasping
Of door hinges,
The barefoot steps at night,
The creaking of a floorboard,
The whisper in an upbeat duo,
The all-embracing sigh.

And in the silent cold,
A midnight hidden moon,
I hear the soft drumming,
A gust of an April breeze.
I sigh with long-remembered joy
Of wishful nights.

And so with tired ears,
I silently lip-read
The melodies, the bridal songs,
Bells, prayers, weeping fiddlers on the roof,
The plainsongs of many days ago.

The Last Applause

It could have been a comedy
Or just an agonizing drama.
The play has ended,
As it once began.

And with the last refrain,
I stand with pen in hand,
My plume, my last salute
To all the actors, all the make-up men.

Now let me take my bow,
No longer fearful of forgotten lines,
The frowning of a prompter,
The ever-present glare of lights.

The accolade, a mere echo from afar,
The curtains fall before my eyes,
Never to rise again—no rose today,
A daisy at my feet, my only prize.

The shuffling feet have ceased,
Torn tickets on the floor,
Attendants waiting at the door,
And silence echoes from the wings.

The Immigrant

Astride his suitcase,
His bronco on the quay,
Impatiently he waits,
The gate of Sesame to spring
And to be ferried
By capricious waves
Of a November stormy sea.

With tired eyes he looks
Upon the sea of dreams,
Down at the water's edge,
The lapping waves,
The blackened sea-encrusted piles,
The screeching gulls,
The shore-born surfers of the wind.

He is the father and the son
Of still-remembered dreams,
Of barren hills, the village stench,
The choking dust,
The wintry frost at night,
But there beyond the water's edge,
A misty sun of hopes had lit the sky,
As yet not fully born.

He wakens from his dreams.
It is a sound, a monody, a wail,
Soft like a song of old,
A summon to embark.
At last his ship had come
Upon the voyage of his dream,
The steamer and the sea,
To take him home.

The Lady on the Isle

"Keep ancient lands, your storied pomp!" cries she
With silent lips. "Give me your tired, your poor,
Your huddled masses yearning to breathe free,
The wretched refuse of your teeming shore.
Send these, the homeless, tempest-tossed to me,
I lift my lamp beside the golden door!"
—Emma Lazarus

Tranquil and serene, the autumn sea,
The rolling of the ship had ceased,
And silently the ship plowed through the morning tide.
The land of our dreams was near,
No longer a delusion, a mirage.

Wrapped in Aurora's mist,
There on the isle the lady stood,
Arm raised, and in her hand
A gilded torch, to light, to greet
The weary voyager, unwanted men—
"The huddled masses," "tempest-tossed,"
The tired and the poor from far away.

By the salt-encrusted rail we stood,
Wounded dreamers of years gone by,
And gazing through the rising mist,
Looked at Bartholdi's mother's somber face,
Read Emma's invite to the shore ahead.
Some read the words, some wept, some smiled.

With license to transform,
I saw the lady once before.
She stood by other open gates,
No torch to greet "beside the golden door."
She stood before me, helmeted, arm raised,
A warrior's sword in hand,
Pale, horror-struck her gentle face.

And as I looked at her,
A prisoner's grateful eye,
I wondered why she came.
What kept her waiting, sword in hand?
And why she came so late
While millions perished,
The hapless victims of a tyrant's hate.

Unpublished Words

At ease the trembling hand,
The faithful pen had ceased to write.
Words born, then cradled on a page,
Become imprisoned thoughts.

Like wing-clipped birds of song
Confined, silent in their cage,
Begging the passersby to read,
Begging to be heard.

Even the mute man sings;
Only his ears can hear the silent chords.
The blind man sees, illumined by an inner light,
A light that none but he alone can see.

So let the words remain at rest
In prose or in poetic rhyme,
For words once formed
Become the obelisks of time.

The Stranger

I knew him once, a friend, a chum of mine.
His grin of youth had given way
To grimace, to a wrinkled brow,
His trembling hand, once master of a pen,
His songs, his words, a blur by now.

He stares, but to his curtained eye,
Milky the dawn, mist-veiled the sunset,
Longer the shadows at day's end—
The pendulum of time is nearly spent.

He was a chance witness
Of much ruin, carnage, floods,
Each ending in a rainbow promise,
While a new deluge followed
Before the last was gone.

A stranger now in a surging crowd,
Adrift he can no longer stem the tide.
With limping gait he shuffles on,
The past a witch's Sabbath,
The future a portentous end.

With pleading eye he shuffles on,
Then hesitates, the man without a name,
A name beyond recall,
A stranger now, a stranger to himself,
A stranger to us all.

The Eyes

Blessed be the eyes
That out of cozy darkness
First saw the light,
Then saw a mother's face.

Blessed be the eyes,
Unfailing servants of the heart,
That bid them to behold
The petal of a rose at dawn.

Eyes, windows of the self,
The wordless orators
Of a thousand idioms
When words begin to fail.

Eyes that gaze within myself,
Sagacious judges on some sunless day,
Knowing to pardon, knowing to absolve
When wisdom and my judgment fail.

Thou Shall Not Kill

"Yummah, Yummah!" Fatima weeps.
"Oh, Allah Acbar!" Our God is great,
Tears streaming down her lacerated face.
"Mayn kind, mayn kind!" Rebecca wails.
"Adonai, eykhod!" Our God is one.
She beats her breasts.
"Rebyata, oy rebiata!" Nadyezhda screams,
"Oh Bozhe moy, oh Bozhe moy!"
"My God, my God!"
And with her fingers claws the frozen tundra soil.

It is their language of despair
For murder of a child,
A child, their flesh, the essence of their being—
Negates the miracle of birth.

And so they lament, so they weep,
Their voices meant to reach
The ears of Allah, Christos, Adonai,
Not men, but man-made Gods,
Gods who have fashioned men.

It is the Gods that lit in some men's breast
The need to torture and to kill,
Purblind, deaf to mother's tears,
It is their morbid thrill.

But there are men who weep with them
And walk and walk with signs aloft.
"Peace on Earth, thou shall not kill,"
Their signs proclaim.

While others, sword in hand
And vengeance in their plumes,
Cry, "War upon such men!"
In time they too will go,
And heeding God's design
With righteousness at heart,
They too will maim and kill.

The Sparrow

We were children, Ben and I,
The world our meadow
To frolic in and romp,
The backyard pond our sea.

Ben grew to be a man,
Tall, unabashed, light-footed,
The world a pageant and he the peacock
With plumage fan in full array,
A dandy man, a popinjay.

One day the knell of time
Struck the senses without
Reason, without rhyme,
In brutal dissonance.

With chin upon his chest,
Ben's speech, a rasping slur,
Bereft of plumage of the years,
His nest with ashes strewn,
A bird of prey, wing-clipped,
A wounded sparrow now.

It Spins

Spinning within its orbit of eternity,
The matins and vespers,
Only illusions made by man,
Invented just to count the time,
To count the cosmic span.

Hiding from the burning sun,
The lustrous sea, the earth,
The wrinkled lands,
The night, an invitation
To recall the day gone by.

Then one more half-turn of the globe,
And dawn dispels the burden of the dark.
A sultry night had given way
To mist-laden droplets on a petal of a rose,
Ushering a newborn, gentle day.

When hope is hope reborn,
Tap dancing and hand clapping,
Garden days in bloom,
The ever-thirsty hummingbirds
In duets with the bumblebees.

And so the earth does turn.
And so does our frame of mind,
The ebbing and the rising of the tide,
Our merriment and past recall
The thoughts of who we were
And who we are today.

The Gates of Hell

Upon the president's visit to Auschwitz
June 1, 2003

Walk gently, for the dust and clay
Still groan with every step of yours
And ask, have you been blind?
Have you been deaf?
When children, naked, hair-shorn, begged,
"I promise to be good,
Just let me live for just one little while,"
And with their parents hand in hand walked to their doom.

Look at the sky, unclouded now,
Azure, unblemished by the clouds
Of smoke, of burning flesh,
The messages to Gods above,
And to those righteous men below,
Of White House lawns, of Downing Street,
The Kremlin and rose gardens.

Look, modern emperors and queens,
At the steely railroad tracks,
Placed there to haul away in cattle cars,
To jettison the detritus,
Believers in a God of long-gone days.
Do not avert your newfound Christian eyes.
Look now and pray.

In Search of Myself

How often have I searched
The road to tell me who I am?
And mystified by many signs,
I wondered where they led.

And then misled, that in the end
All roads led somewhere.
The safest one to take
Would be the road into myself.

Homeward bound, it led,
Weather-beaten, rock-strewn,
Sun-splashed, familiar footprints
Showing me the way.

I trudged along, foot-sore,
Parched and with tired leg,
The horizon of my aim
Receding with each step.

And when I got there by and by,
Tired and with halting breath,
The road came to an end.
"Stop here and gaze!"
A full-length mirror said.

The image convoluted, warped,
Bandy-legged, a grinning clown,
Clodhoppers on my feet,
A spooky apparition, stood I,
Half tearful and half smile.

And so I stood and realized
It simply wasn't worth the effort.
It simply wasn't worth the time.
The image wasn't I,
Or was it?

Imagination

I dreamed I was the king of kings,
A wealthy potentate,
My royal residence a treasure trove
Of things I gathered one by one
By means of amity, by means of wars.

A lifelong aggregate
Of precious gems,
Of sculpted handiwork,
The silks of distant lands,
My floors were gilded tiles

Exquisite art adorned my walls
To fit my opulent abode.
Pure golden was my scepter and my crown,
My robe, silk-woven,
And at my side a ceremonial sword.

Soft silken were my cushions
To entice and to allure
An Eve, a Venus, an Aphrodite,
To quench my longing arms
If only for a single tryst.

Then startled by an avian song
I suddenly woke up to realize
No brocade cushion there;
My head is resting on the bark
Of my shade-giving tree.

My treasures though are there,
The ruby is my crimson summer rose,
Gold dust residing in my lily's heart,
The silken moss, a damsel's soft caress,
The ferns and spiderwebs my filigrees.

Sweet berries,
The blue jays and the mockingbirds—
One my court jester, the other one my bard—
Tall stand my hollyhocks and glads,
My ever-faithful royal guards.

My crown, a straw hat now,
The denim overalls, my royal gown,
The cutters, hoe, the wooden rake,
The workmen's leather gloves,
My scepter and the mace.

It is the realm of open gates,
No drawbridge and no moats,
No ramparts and no canons here,
The garden is my sovereignty,
And here I sway supreme.

To Rest, To Sleep

"To sleep: perchance to dream …"
—William Shakespeare, *Hamlet*

Rest at ease, the faithful pen,
Even the tallest elm at season's end
Must shed its leaves.
The mighty bear, the lion in his den,
Must hibernate to gather strength
To rule supreme again.

They say the spirit,
Like the most fertile soil,
Must be permitted to lie fallow,
To be fruitful once again.
The windblown seed
Embedded in its womb
Must find its heart and learn to throb.

The bard's most joyous song must end,
And so the writer's hand
Needs to desist, or else
His rhymes turn formless, shallow,
His thoughts a parched and arid land,
And the most nimble fingers
Must cease to pluck the harp.

Awakened by the drifting wind,
The sleeping butterfly unfolds its wings.
The night to dream is gone,
And born again it heeds the call
And heads for home again.
The writer's pen, stirred from its sleep,
Begins to scribble in half-dream.

The Thirteenth Chime

The clock struck suddenly again,
The thirteenth beat, harsh,
Unlike the others, a deadly knell,
An alien chime, pain-racked,
Gripped by a crushing fear.

The limelight dimmed,
And suddenly a gloomy dusk
Eclipsed the shadows on my moonlit stage.
The wheels of time began to slow.
The gears of all my being ceased to mesh.

They slowed but didn't cease to turn,
And all the rivers ceased to flow.
The road ahead had reached its end.
"Nothing beyond," the road sign said,
And with my lips compressed,
Silently I begged, *Not yet, not yet.*

With a pain-constricted throat,
I was the beggar, begging for some alms,
For just another day,
A grant, an offering, a gift of stay,
But there was stillness.

A spark lit far away,
Soft whispers, fluttering of lips
Of other aproned men,
All gazing at a glassy screen.

A man's face hidden by a mask,
A guiding catheter in hand,
I felt the ebbing of my pain
And stillness of the night
Gave rise to a soft tune of rippling waves.
The river flowed again.

He spoke, "Look, look, it beats
A normal rhythm. It's back again"—
A whisper with a solemn ring,
Tough to my empty ears. It was a shout;
I knew it all too well.
They spoke of life and death.

In doubt whose life was on the scale,
Light flooded once again the darkened stage.
The pain was gone, and I perceived
That life grew wings, my river flowed again,
And she stood there. The guardian beyond the screen
Was there to watch, to nurture, to sustain.

The Lover

I've seen you make love
Wherever you wished,
On an ice-covered pond
Or soft green moss.

On the sidewalk,
In the backyard, or in the middle of the street,
In the neighbor's flower bed,
None too discreet.

At sunrise or at dusk,
A sunlit sky or a full moon,
You lady-killer, Don Juan,
At midnight or high noon.

Be she brunette with ringlet hair,
Voluptuous, dainty-legged,
Or with the shape of a teddy bear,
You love them just the same.

And in your tryst you do not care,
Softly caressed, love-bitten in the neck,
As long as it is she
Who gives a heck.

You part without adieu,
With a lusty bark and waggling tail.
You pounce upon your Alpo dish,
You sexy hero of the day.

Professor Le Roach

As Professor Le Roach,
It is my duty to teach
As best as I know,
Without bias or slightest reproach,
The story of humans of eons ago.

A biped, and of brittle skin,
Sans wings, sans antennae, sans grace,
Abhorrent, hateful was his grin
On his sordid humanoid face
As he sought our doom
With his foot and his broom.

Homo sapiens, he called himself.
Homo what? with doubt do I say.
And as I look at the past,
I fervently hope, I fervently pray,
He's been gone forever,
Gone, vanished at last.

Look back at his Gods at hand.
One sat in the shade of a tree,
Another one armed with a magic wand,
A master of plagues and the parting sea,
A fisherman wrapped in a shroud,
A camel man and his angel with wings,
And at last the great mushroom cloud.

The last one filling the sky,
Erasing the sun in its fiery path,
And in a flash like the flip of a wing of a fly,
Man's reign was finished,
Gone without saying as much as good-bye.

We're free now, three cheers and hooray,
Six-legged brethren with feathered antennae,
Walking with stealth in brown camouflage,
No need to hide any longer, no need to flee,
Beneath a cupboard or the creaking stair.

And so at dawn as you leave your den,
Raise your head and fold your wings.
Gaze with awe at the sky,
And with a murmur fervently pray,
For there resides our king of all kings,
The great cockroach with his fiery eye,
And tired at night our mother the moon
Takes her turn as she softly glides by.

I Know You

I know the throb of your heart,
The drumbeat echoes
Of so many words unspoken,
Words winged and words sublime,
Unspoken still at dawn,
Merely a hush at eventide,
But in the stillness of the night
Uttered with every sigh.

I know the sculpture of your thighs,
Unseen but mirrored in each step,
The soft-curved breasts
With every breath,
The ebbing and the falling tide,
The nodding of your head
In cadence with your thoughts,
In silent discourse with yourself.

And yet the many thoughts
You harbor in the safety
Of the source of life,
The fig leaf mystery,
Pandora's gifts of pain and hope—
These I shall never know,
So let it be, for you are woman
And I am only man.

  196

The Gourmand

I am the nibbler of good food,
A guzzling, swilling bon vivant,
The finger-licking epicure
Of chicken à la king
And chicken cacciatore.

But best of all, I like the chicken
Strutting down the dusty road,
Worm picking, cackling,
The wing-spread chick,
The morning cockatoo.

The picker, dainty feeder,
With lusty eye I ogle
Fresh roasted ham,
Orange-glazed spareribs.

And yet how fondly I behold
My porcine, squealing friend,
Gazing at me with beady eye
In its malodorous and dingy sty.

With trembling hand I cut
The juicy T-bone steak,
Garlic-refined beef provençale,
Grilled, roasted, even stewed.

And yet in quest of tranquil moods
I like my beef upon the lea,
The tail-swishing kind,
Its plaintive sunrise moo.

The skewered cubes of lamb,
Grilled, marinated chops,
The cutlets and the stew
A glutton's ecstasy, a sheer delight.

And yet my eye prefers to feast
Upon the rolling hills,
The romping ewes and rams,
And listen to their baas.

Bel Canto

So much of our lives are songs,
Some our own, some borrowed,
Like mockingbirds, the mime,
Slavish in semblance and disguise.

A rocking cradle lullaby
To still a thirsty infant's cry,
A toddler's bandy-legged walk
And squeal of joy.

A young boy's lusty yell,
The rumpled hair,
The wings upon his restless feet,
The sky, the wind his heir.

The trumpet call to walk,
To march in step to be alike,
The head held high
In martial stride.

A dandy's whistle
In his evening prowl,
A wedding march,
A softly whispered vow.

And later on a dirge,
A sorrowful regret,
A friend once prospered
And died in pain.

I sing my song,
A not too softly chiming bell,
Mine is a coda of the past,
Not yet a farewell.

The Listener

I've ceased to listen to the thunder
Of waves pounding, crashing
Over moss-covered boulders,
Lashed by sun-dried weeds,
Waves heaving, surging against
The rocky shores of yesterdays.

Now I only hear the mist-wrapped,
Moonlit whispers of a tranquil sea,
The rasping melody of sand,
Faint echoes of a conch,
The cries of a lonely albatross,
Skimming the cresting waves.

In my half dream of long ago,
Free of terror, free of fear,
Perceived by fading ears,
Lip-reading I can only hear
The snare-drum song,
The ebbing tide.

That Ole Man River

Quiet runs my river,
No longer winding, twisting,
Mountain streams
Peaceful and tranquil now.

Unspent the foaming waves,
Tired and chilled,
Autumnal leaves adrift,
Reluctantly it flows
Upon the gathered silt.

In river-dream recall
Of chafing, rushing waves
Through gorges, canyons
Chilled by crumbling glaciers,
Then warmed by pelting rains.

Soft waters once,
Then bittersweet,
Once halted by a dam,
Then freed again
And joined by other streams.

Nearly home and spent,
It spreads its swanlike wings
To brace horizons, tranquil sea,
To be reborn in its domain,
To dream again.

And like that ole man river,
He don't say nothin',
But must know somethin'.
He just keeps rollin'.
He just keeps rollin' along.

To Be Alive

While day by day and often
During sleepless nights,
We gaze with half-averted eyes.
Without much sorrow, without a tear,
We look upon the sallow skin,
Upon the somnolent, the sunken cheeks,
The swollen belly of a child.

The raging hate, the villages on fire,
The maimed, the crippled,
Charred remnant of a dwelling,
Bomb shredded, stained attire,
The ravaged and the raped,
Begging for mercy, asking for help.

So raise your chalice, doff your hat,
Sing praise to Dante's hell.
Drink up, drink up, my fellow man.
Drink up, be calm,
Your remedy, your balm,
While others lower caskets,
And in their idioms whisper, "Dust to dust,"
Into the earthen realm.

Must I Forget?

"There is no remembrance of former things;
Neither shall there be any remembrance of things
That are to come with those that shall come after."
—Ecclesiastes 1:11

At last the sun has set,
The night about to spawn,
Perhaps reluctant of another dawn.
The past is set to take its flight
On wings of evanescence.

Must I, the weary wanderer,
Forget the cradlesong,
The wind-born lilts of yesterday,
The mesmerizing pendulum,
Pacemaker to my daily life?

Must I forget a mother's lilt,
Cradling her newborn against her milk-ripe breasts,
The schoolboy's restless feet beneath the bench,
The sparrow on the windowsill
In duet with the teacher at the desk?

Or the first rays at dawn,
Mist-laden shafts of light,
Skipping over the rippling brook,
Two butterflies, two snowflakes
In their summer flight.

The hoofbeat sound,
The early morning milkman's cart
Over the wooden bridge,
The old man snapping whip,
His sleepy urging slang.

The throaty chanting of a frog
Concealed within a clump of reed,
And then another one, the caw
Of the black raven,
Of tear-stained days, of days of awe.

And then another song,
The blessing on a cup of wine,
The shattered glass, a blushing bride,
Soft whispers in the night,
The whimper of a hungry child.

Gaudeamus, as we rejoice,
Clad in a borrowed cap and gown,
A smile with head held high,
A necklace stethoscope,
A steady hand and well-trained eye.

Must I forget a grandchild's
Tinny song, the garlands from afar?
These are the sounds of my delights,
Beyond erase of time,
Etched and indelible these sights.

Delusions

Strutting upon a trembling soil,
The fire just beneath our feet,
We think we are the masters,
Full of confidence, full of conceit.

Without feathered wings we fly.
Without gills we swim, we dive,
Self-appointed rulers of the sea, the sky,
The larks at dawn, the bats at night.

But we are only butterflies of time,
A flash, the blinking of an eon's eye,
A speck,
A bit of dust in the cosmic sky.

We are the windblown kites,
Intoxicated by our might,
Adorned with hope
In our heedless flight.

Without ears attuned
To the shifting currents
Of all prevailing moral storms,
Wind-driven we remain afloat.

And yet we all are tethered
To a hand as yet unknown.
Unknowingly we drift, we err,
Into the coming bliss or blight.

And so pretending
We must sing,
Recite our mantras,
Inveterate dreamers
Of a promised land.

Of Doubt

Who set the clock
Of night and day,
A clock that never went astray?

Who swirled the electrons,
Then set them in their spin,
And multiplied their kin?

Who ruled that silver
Tarnishes in time,
But gold must always shine?

Who ruled that daffodils
Must wilt at summer's drought,
While other flowers sprout?

Who ruled that stones we trod upon
Or pass them by forever last,
But men must ail and all must die?

Who ruled that every spring
A rose is born according to some plan,
While other seeds will make a man?

Let Not the Children Die

Let not the howling dogs of hunger
Be an infant's cradlesong.
Let not the desert flies
Forever quench their thirst
In children's eyes.

Come, all you sons and daughters
Of the crescent scimitar,
The holy cross,
The lotus man,
The blue-white star.

Your tears alone,
Your songs of woe,
Your wringing hands
Will not abate the hunger
Of a single child.

No rubies, gilded diadems
Will seed the arid desert soil,
Will bring the rains,
Will make ancient rivers flow
Through sandy desert lands.

The swollen bellies,
The outstretched hands
To Gods will not suffice,
Nor the soft whimper,
Nor the lament, nor the sigh.

No drumbeat, tenor, no cantata
Will ever feed a hungry child,
For it is white-robed man
With turban from another clan
That kills the seed
And kills the infant in its mother's arm.

My Seven Deadly Sins

While some were born to sainthood,
Their halos like a miner's lamp,
Casting light wherever they walk,
Flash-warning of each tempting snare,
Righteously they trod along
Their hallowed saintly paths.

I, for one, was born to sin,
And as I walk with crooked stealth,
No halo floats above my head,
Only a burglar's lamp
With hardly a flicker of light.

I hear the angels
Play their gilded harps,
Flapping their wings serenely.
I stand in silence,
Catlike sly in my disguise.

Bare-bottom, rubicund,
They pluck their little harps,
Falsetto-voiced sing their hosannas,
But I stomp my feet,
I kick my legs, I clap my hands,
My face an everlasting grin.

I laugh at them and thumb my nose.
Mine is a virtue that they lack
In poetry or prose.
I am the pleasure man,
The matchless paragon
Of all the seven deadly sins.

The Time Has Come

The time has come to be at ease,
The nameless voyager of yesterday,
Once rootless without home,
Foot-sore, the wanderer,
Stumbling along with tired sway
Along the dusty country roads,
The fugitive, the runaway.

The time has come to cease
To dream of wings,
Of ornate feathers in my hat,
Of gazing at the signposts,
Of promises betrayed,
Of once upon a time,
Of roads I strayed.

The time has come
To be at ease at last,
Inhale the fragrant scent
Of springtime trees abloom,
And dream along the shifting
Clouds of wishful thoughts,
And to forget the heartbreak days
Of things that should have been,
The days that now are naught.

Know Thyself

I am the fisherman, the angler,
Tireless seeker.
I am the quarry,
Short-lived, ephemeral,
My pen the fishing rod,
My quest the evanescent lure
To find at last, to know
Of who I am.

The river, the pebbly shore,
And down below,
Beneath the rippling waves,
Swiftly and with stealth flit by.
My life,
In ever-changing flow,
Escapes my searching eye.

The sun has set,
Gilding the rippling waves.
Empty now,
Exhausted is my pen.
My vision dimmed,
Long and illusive the shadows
Of who I think I am.

And so each day
I cast anew my line
Into the ever-changing stream,
For I was told
That I must find myself,
And so I fish.
I fish and wonder why.

The Ballad of the Missing Rib

Opening my eyes at dawn,
I stretched my limbs,
And with a big yawn
I realized with sinking heart
That part of me took flight,
Had simply gone.

One rib had vanished in my dream,
Gone, snatched from me,
Robbed, stolen without my consent,
Capriciously by an unknown hand,
A deed I couldn't understand.

With full resolve to get it back
By any means was my intent.
Down Eden Street I went,
The serpent basking in the sun
With a sly grin just shook his head.

The bearded scholar, staff in hand,
Ceased writing, lost in thought,
Then shrugged, and turning
To the tablets in his lap
Continued scribbling once again.

And so I walked and walked
Until I came upon a stream,
And in the shade a maiden sat,
A loaf of bread, a jug of wine,
A paintbrush in her hand.
Her name was Thou,
And so we sat to chat.

Sloe-eyed, crimson lips, and fair,
Lithesome and raven-black hair,
It set my heart aflutter.
I tasted of her wine and some,
And all I could utter was a stutter.

Beneath the silken canopy we stood.
Roses of Sharon, her face was veiled
From the cup of wine we took a sip
While the preacher spoke his last refrain:
"I now pronounce you Man and Rib,"
And I was whole again.

Let the Wounds Heal

Let silence fall upon the past,
Sever the shackles and the bonds,
The yoke, the heavy burden,
The twilight shadows cast.

Bid farewell to what
Unwilling eyes beheld.
Erase the echoes
Of the anguished cries.

Let heal the wounds of yesterdays,
The hidden sores,
Those camouflaged,
Concealed by smiles.

And while your eyes
Still search in vain
For comfort in the rippling waves,
In an elusive mountain stream.

Abandon fear,
The stream no longer tinged
By crimson waves,
Now crystal clear.

The clatter of the wheels
Upon the wooden bridge,
It is the milkman's horse
No longer stepping hobnailed heels.

The nettle weeds
Have lost their sting.
The dandelions' milky sap
Turned sweet again.

In Praise of Sound

I still can hear
The flutter of a hummingbird,
The chirping sparrow in its flight,
The springtime raindrop songs
Upon my roof at night.

I pray let not the silence
Of the spheres beyond,
The hush of everlasting nights,
Erase the cooing of a newborn babe,
The playful laughter of a child.

Let not the hush of sleep,
Eternal sleep bereft of sound,
Efface the avian plaintive melodies
And fervent whispers in the night.

Let me still hear the vibrant
Resonance of cello strings,
The echoes of a far-off thunder,
The droning of a bumblebee,
The flutter of its wings.

Let me remain the man of songs,
With words, with pen,
Before the clock of time
Has run its course
Into eternal nights.

Ashes to Ashes

"Do not go gentle into that good night
… rage, rage against the dying of the light."

No, Dylan Thomas,
Go and rage
If you so wish.
I have no time to fume,
To vent my ire,
To kick, to trash,
To set my soul on fire.

No, Dylan Thomas,
No, not me, I shall be busy
Watching autumn leaves
Fall to their wintry ground
In silence of the coming night
To where we all are bound.

No, Dylan Thomas,
To rage, to rant? you said.
I shall be way too busy
To gather all the gifts of life
Received with our neonatal cry,
First smile, first frown,
First laughter, and first tear.

I shall be too busy to recall
Some best forgotten,
Some to be sung in rhythm and rhyme,
Some in a tenor grosso,
Some in a silent hum.

And having wished adieu
To stormy days of years gone by,
I shall gift wrap the rainbow,
The one to never flood again,
Only a chunk of it, a thimbleful,
Only a bit of the setting sun
Before it dips below the crest,
A fragment of an ogling moon,
A star, and all the rest.

In my falsetto voice
That none but I can hear,
I shall declaim
God bless an eagle's wing,
A fluttering stripe
Of red and blue and white,
A greeting lady by the sea,
Holding a torch,
A greeting issued just for me.

And when at last I close my eyes,
Let ashes to ashes, in ashes' idiom,
Whisper, let him be the man he was,
Dull at times or bright,
And let no kaddish be my elegy—
Only the giggle of a little child.

The Dreamer

I dreamed I was the king of kings,
A wealthy potentate,
My royal residence a treasure trove
Of things I gathered one by one
By means of amity, by means of wars.

A lifelong aggregate
Of precious gems,
Of sculpted handiwork,
The silks of distant lands,
My floors were gilded tiles

Exquisite art adorned my walls
To fit my opulent abode.
Pure golden was my scepter and my crown,
My robe, silk-woven,
And at my side a ceremonial sword.

Soft silken were my cushions
To entice and to allure
An Eve, a Venus, an Aphrodite,
To quench my longing arms
If only for a single tryst.

Then startled by an avian song
I suddenly woke up to realize
No brocade cushion there.
My head is resting on the bark
Of my shade-giving tree.

My treasures though are there,
The ruby is my crimson summer rose,
Gold dust residing in my lily's heart,
The silken moss, a damsel's soft caress,
The ferns and spiderwebs my filigrees.

Sweet berries
And the mockingbirds,
One my court jester, the other one my bard,
Tall stand my hollyhocks and glads,
My ever-faithful royal guards.

My crown, a straw hat now,
The denim overalls, my royal gown,
The cutters, hoe, the wooden rake,
The workmen's leather gloves,
My scepter and the mace.

It is the realm of open gates,
No drawbridge and no moats,
No ramparts and no canons here,
The garden is my sovereignty,
And here I sway supreme.

My blissful reverie
Still clinging to my tired eyes,
And as I look with awe,
I wonder, was it all a dream,
Or am I dreaming now?

The Fiddler on the Roof

Old man, you bard of yesterday,
Each day from sunrise until dusk
You sat there on the roof
Bestowing melodies,
The sustenance of those of want,
To soothe all those in sorrow,
To give them hope
When hope became extant.

You played your tunes
While in the narrow village lanes.
The children sang
And barefoot kicked the dust,
The cackling chicken, lowing cows,
A rural symphony a ballad
As rich or as poor as life bestows.

And you looked down,
And crinkly-eyed you smiled,
The melodies a rosin to you bow,
To softly glide upon
The strings in rhythm and rhyme.

It didn't last forever, though,
For then one day
You gazed at those below
And saw the empty dusty roads.
The listeners down below were gone,
And suddenly you ceased to play.

It was a day
Of sorrow and of gloom,
The fiddle still beneath your chin,
The nimble bow devoid of strings,
And flail your arm
And trembling hand,
Tears flowing down your beard.

Gone were the lilting songs,
The once dulcet melodies,
Replaced by pealing bells,
By shouts of discord.
Run, run, my children.
Run, run, and hide
Before it is too late.

He disappeared, the fiddle man,
His fiddle now a dream,
Or could it have been
A fantasy, the melody
That wafted through the air,
A melody of sadness, joy,
Without a trace forever gone?

Self-Portrait

Dim the memory
Of that first blush of being,
The halting steps,
The fledgling years
Of slingshot, bow and arrow,
Swashbuckling days
Of make-believe and daring.

How wistfully I grope
For the once nimble wings
That kept me aloft
of strife.

Dream wings they were,
Now shorn,
Clipped one by one
By the tempests of time,
Bent, stoop-shouldered now,
Unsteady my walk,
Lines drawn upon my brow.

A blur, my penmanship,
I write, I hesitate, I start anew
In search of meaning,
Of relevance of words,
My syntax, sentences askew.

But pen in hand
In days of doubt
Of who I am,
Before I become stranger
To myself,
I look upon my child
And I am blessed,
A ray of morning light
Upon his smiling face,
And wonder why the quest.

Delusion

Strutting upon the trembling soil,
The fire just beneath our feet,
We are the self-deluded fumblers,
Full of confidence, full of conceit.

Without feathered wings we fly.
Without gills or fins we swim, we dive.
We are the rulers of the sea, the sky,
The larks at dawn, the bats at night.

We are the butterflies of time,
The blinking of an eon's eye,
An evanescent speck, a mote,
The dust in cosmic mist.

The windblown kites, we are
Intoxicated by our heights,
Adorned with hopes
In our heedless flights.

With our ears tuned into
Whimsies of all the currents we gloat,
Of all prevailing storms,
Wind-driven we remain afloat.

Yet tethered we all are
To a hand as yet unknown,
And so we blunder
Into tomorrow's still unknown.

And so pretending
To be one and all,
Self-deluded do we sing
Te Deum and hosannas,
And to our hopes we cling.

To Notice

I noticed the wind
By the flutter of aspen leaves,
The biting cold
By the flushed cheeks of a smiling child.

I noticed the rain
In the splashing of a passing car,
The tortoise shells of umbrellas
The quick-stepping passerby.

I noticed the passing of time
By the tremor of my hand,
The many lines across my brow,
The missing leaves from my calendar.

I noticed the pain
In the near emptiness
Of my medicine vial,
The puffy eyelids of unsleeping nights.

The Wanderer

By some capricious genesis
I've become a snowflake,
Swirling afloat, windblown,
Beating my crystal wings.

The butterfly of winter—
I search, I seek to find
A perch within the spirals
Of a winter's gale
To stay suspended
Amid the heavens.

Created by the whim
Of northern currents,
Wintry gales, some distant shore,
And ever-changing tides of air,
I flutter, I soar.

I live and yet I know
That soon I too shall fall
And down on earth
Commingle with my sister flakes
To be the mantle of white snow.

But not yet shall I die.
First I shall add
A sparkle to the frosty earth,
To all the crystals,
The wintry canopy of life.

And when the sun shall rise,
Our summon to return
From where we came,
I and my sister flakes
Will readily obey.

Although trodden down,
I shall rise once again,
Of snowy ashes born
To soar, to soar, to soar.

To Atone

Give me back my wings so I can fly
Across the span of time
And look upon the years gone by.

So I can fly once more
And in my retrospective flight
Gaze at the hurt, the pain,
The sorrow-laden sight,
Wing-beat my breast in penance
Before it is too late to fly.

On Writing Poems

There are days when words,
Law-abiding, amenable of sorts,
Come to life in perfect rhyme.

There are fallow, rainy days,
Each word a silent man with shuffling feet.

Words frosty, chilling, the skies dark,
Lame men standing in line,
Waiting before a closed door of the mind,
Waiting and not knowing why.

Then comes the day of sunlit words,
Light, brisk, a child hopping on one leg,
A soaring butterfly capricious in its flight,
A jingle full of rhythm and rhyme.

And I, the juggler and the mime,
Stand mute, my eyes half-closed and then
My words walk by, tiptoeing slowly or in haste,
And I stand there to offer them my pen.

Noah and the Deluge

Look out there, Noah,
See what God has wrought,
To try his genesis anew.
Capriciously he drowned all men,
Sparing only animals and you.

Stay hidden, Noah, in your hand-hewn ark;
The time to leave is not at hand.
The only bird on Ararat, a raven bird of doom,
It is a dove in camouflage, all white.

Beware, the bird of your delusion
Is merely a bird of prey,
The olive branch, a deadly hemlock bough,
Not the proverbial gift of peace.

Its flight is not the tiding of goodwill;
It is a flight of terror
At what your God has done,
His caw, a stifled sob, a cry.

It's winter, Noah,
The birds of peace are still to come.
The spring is far away.

Alone on Ararat, your gift of speech
No animal could fathom.
God drowned all men.
To be forever silent is your bane.

Look out there, Noah, take another drink.
Look at the giant rainbow far away.
It's not a covenant, old man.
It's only one more gate to hell.

The Historical Apple Tree

Lulled by the shade
Of my apple tree,
I rest against the verdant trunk,
Gaze at my sun-bracing friends
With awe and love, half-drunk,
And speak to them in apple words.

I see you there, old friend of mine, red-cheeked,
You temptress apple, the serpent's swain,
Alluring, beckoning with wily reptile words.
You were the cause for men to toil
And women to bear men in labor pain.

And you there, clutching with your stem
The drooping, tired branch,
The apple Paris gave to Aphrodite
In Hella's contest of the Gods,
The cause of strife, the cause of blight.

And over there, concealed by leaves,
You impudent and brazen thing
That woke old Newton from his sleep
To let him know why man must walk
And birds must fly on a wing.

Don't hide beneath the drooping branch.
Look at the sun with pride,
The William Tells of apple tale,
Guiding his arrow
To see his child free from assail.

And you, the bashful,
Sun-kissed fruit beneath that other branch,
A loving mother's apple of her eye,
The way she gazes at her babe,
Suckling at her breast to still its cry.

Fat, luscious apple near the pinnacle above,
Don't brag so much, don't glow
By being the quintessence of America,
The content of cold cider,
Of motherhood and pie.

And you up there, so proud,
You apple of invention,
Playmate of Macintosh and Macs,
Of dot-coms and of rams,
Minus a byte from your dimension.
And you the shameless apple,
To be partaken once a day,
A doctor's bane, the illness's foe,
The guardian of man's health,
Another covenant man must obey.

And all the rest of you with crimson cheeks,
And you, the paler ones within the canopy of leaves,
The wormy, pockmarked, pincushions for a hungry beak,
Soon I shall pluck you too,
My dreamer's apples on my tree.

Confessions

I ain't no poet, no rhymer, and no bard,
Only a doodler
On the margins of my daily life.

Ain't got no magic
In my threadbare sleeves,
No stovepipe hat,
No tricks, no subterfuge.

I'm only a pickpocket
On the loose,
A restless vagrant,
Stealing a word here and there.

A panhandler squatting
On the sidewalk grate,
Hand outstretched, palm up,
Begging for a thought.

But on a sandy shore,
A starlit night,
Alone and swaddled
In the blanket of my past.

Unbidden and unasked-for
Words come at last,
Rushing at me with the tide.

Of Sounds

Dawn enters through the murky autumn panes,
A naked maple branch sun-kissed aglow,
My wake-up call, the end of dreams,
In slow and gentle tremolo.

The days are short, the nights too long,
The tardy eastern sky, a thespian on the stage
Reluctant to read his lines
In hesitant ritardando.

The summits of the trees light up,
Ablaze like Sabbath candles
In sprightly scherzo.

Down in the street and wide awake,
The milkman's wheels
Rattle on the cobbled pavement stones
In ragtime beat accelerando.

The church bells rend the silence,
Loud and overwhelming
In shrill vibrato.

The drumbeat on the wooden stairs,
The schoolboy's footsteps,
Late for school again,
In swift staccato.

My sloe-eyed next-door neighbor sings,
Soft voiced, the same refrain,
Rehearsing for the night
In soft bel canto.

The day drifts by,
My hands upon the keyboard
Speed up, then slow again
In largo or andante chord.

Night calls upon my nodding head,
The pillow sings my lullaby,
A nocturne for the hunter in the sky.

Circus

Come, enter my enticing circus tent
Of flimflam, fallacy, and delusions.
Look at the fat lady prancing on the stage,
Her bulging cheeks, her hair brick red,
While in the alleyway a hungry child
Begs for a crumb of bread.

Look, the clown is standing on his head,
His baggy pants, his floppy shoes,
Look, clap your hands and smile,
While out there thousands weep.

Look at the doggy on its hind legs,
A blue ball balanced on its muzzle,
And doves of peace aflutter at the apex of the tent,
A man suspended by his plait,
While in the town square in neat rows
Stand men with polished boots and wait.

Dance

Dance with me,
My arms still strong,
While hand in hand we touch,
Our feet in duet song.

Dance with me,
Become my rhythm, become my rhyme,
And dancing let us be
The tumbling mountain brook
Before we turn
Into the calm and placid sea.

Before the winter comes
To claim the lustfulness
Of youthful limbs
And gold turns into silver crowns.

Our frowns, our smiles become deep etched
Upon our brow,
Our eyes unclouded yet,
Our ears attuned to whispers in the night.

Let us dance with grace
While days are longer than a wintry night
And our breaths remain
A pleasure's sigh.

Sleep, My Child

Sleep, my child,
Rest against my breast.
The sandman's at the gate.
Your eyes are heavy.
The hour is late.

Sleep, dream, your prince resides
In his palace on the hill,
The marble floor,
A thousand candles lit,
The music plays.

Sleep, do not gaze
Upon the earthen floor,
Adobe walls, the barren shelves,
The howling of the hungry wolves.
Let not the biting wind
Become your cradlesong.

Dream on, my child,
For all your dreams
Someday will come to naught.
Princes, palaces are a disguise,
And all the fairy tales
Of lands of milk and honey
Are only man-made lies.

The Echo Man

I am the echo man without a voice my own,
My granite molecules receiving sound
Deep etched by winds of time.
Mute witness to the trials of man,
I am the chronicle in pantomime.

They say that in the end all echoes die,
Dwindle, join others, fade
Out there, where silence of eternity,
The graveyard of all sound,
Stands ready to receive, ready for decay.

I say it isn't so,
For I believe that somewhere
In that realm of Milky Ways,
The echoes meet again and sort themselves
By sound, by volume, and content.

And thus reborn, reshaped, resound once more,
And those attuned to cosmic sounds,
Unknowing from where they came,
Will listen to the past and forge them into now.

The Buccaneer of Lincoln High

You braved the stormy seas.
A gale had snapped the mast.
Your shipmate, your best friend,
Into the raging waves was cast.

You are the strutting buccaneer,
Tarrying in harbors of exotic lands,
Of half-clad damsels, almond eyes,
Shrill whistles, tambourines, and wailing chants.

At last, with tattered sails,
You're home again after so many years,
The salty breeze still in your hair,
The echo of the hurricane still in your ears.

Put back the rapier, buccaneer,
Into the gem-encrusted scabbard.
Desist now from your infamous career.
You're home, past your travails.

Your math homework is still not done,
The garbage pail unemptied by the door,
Your bed unmade, your hair is still unkempt,
The school bus on its way.

Come, get your chocolate, for it is late.
You're safe now, Mama's gangly buccaneer.
You've dueled, killed, and looted.
It's over now, intrepid musketeer.

And cease to frown your acned brow,
For there are seven seas as yet to sail,
A million men to match your blade,
Mountains galore for you to scale.

And so much time is left,
Intrepid buccaneer,
So dream and dream and while you do
You better hurry up, the bus is here.

There Was a Time

There were days to remember,
Days full of darkness, the sun eclipsed by fear,
Cataclysmic days when men
Dared not to look, had to avert their gaze,
Days of alarm, days of dismay,
Death using the palette of death to paint itself
With the facsimile of men.

I try to erase them, trample on,
Burn the unwanted pages,
The calendar of all too many days,
Turn a mute ear to the harsh sounds,
And listen only to the harmony of song.

To look at faces and be blind
To all the scars there etched
By acids of the many tears,
Shed by so many, some vanished now,
And all those left behind.

The World Is a Stage

The world is a stage,
And we, unwitting actors
In our life's allotted time.
We are obliged, we must attend,
Strut back and forth,
Gesturing, reciting in prose or rhyme
By means of words, by means of song,
By signals or by pantomime.

At times I was compelled to watch the play,
Allotted to a front row seat.
Agog and full of wonder did I gaze,
But there were times when troubled by the glare
Of the bright floodlights,
The hullabaloo, the loud fanfare,
I sought a seat way in the rear,
Along with others overcome by fright.

Some in the audience clapped,
Others hooted, some even cheered,
A catcall here and there,
Some dared to hiss, some even wept,
And to this day, aghast by what I saw,
I keep on wondering with pity and dismay
Who was the playwright
And why this gory play.

To My Heirs

To you
I bequeathed the throb of my heart,
The depth of my breath,
My temper, and my calm.

I gave you my shape,
My face, demeanor, pride,
The mettle to endure,
The feebleness to fail.

My patrimony I bestowed
To you, unwary child,
To praise when all went well,
At other times to chide.

Being the heir of gifts ,
I too bestow unasked-for alms,
As someday you in turn
Will do the same.

And like the never-changing tide,
Its ebb and flow,
We all receive and then bestow
The gist of who we are.

The Newcomer

Swathed, bundled up, tightfisted it arrives,
The hairless bundle of pink flesh,
Forever thirsty, suckling, screaming at full throat.
Cross-eyed it squirms in our arms,
And we, agog, call it the great hope.

You wanted me, it seems to say.
Was it a carnival, a spree of lust,
A drunken revelry, a feast of love?
Too late, it says, it matters not,
Now take me as I am.

The Chase

He was a boy with scabs on his knees,
With unkempt hair and running nose,
Smudges of dirt tattoos on his chin,
Scuffed shoes, his pants too short.

His pockets bulged with marbles,
Dried chestnuts, flat pebbles,
A piece of twine, a twisted nail,
A treasure trove of magic rings.

Smooth river-polished bits of glass,
A slingshot with one broken tine,
A pocketknife with half a blade,
An unripe apple, a stolen plum.

He was a boy with wings,
Full of disdain to walk.
He took to the air with every step,
Carried aloft by the wind.

A champion catcher of pollywogs
And other crawling things,
He wrestled lions,
Chased eagles in the sky.

And then one day the boy was on the run,
Chased by a man with silver hair,
A limping man, brandishing a cane,
Waving his arm, gasping for a bit of air.

A dreamer man, he too was on the run,
Pursuing the boy he once had been,
Pursuing and yelling with a faltering voice,
"Wait for me, my boy, please wait."

"Once I was you," he shouted from afar.
"Oh, let me be the boy again.
Please, let me be the boy you are,
If only for a single day."

To Worship

Men worshipped God, who spoke to them
From a mountaintop in the wilderness of Shem,
God's voice, the burning bush,
Commandments etched in stone
By the desert-swirling sands.

And in the shadow of a tree
There sat another man,
A former nobleman, a loincloth now his garb,
Hands resting in his lap,
And on his lips an enigmatic smile.

One spoke from the top of a pyramid,
Steps crimson with his victim's blood,
His priests in gilded gowns,
Disguised half canine and half men,
The gilded serpent as their crowns.

One spoke with the knell of a thunder,
Another with the roar of the sea,
Or in the icy chill of the northern wind,
Some form the lofty Mount Olympus
Or the halls of Valhalla.

Mine spoke to me clad in a prayer shawl,
A man-made tent enfolding him
From head down to his heels,
And I, his grandson, with rapt ear
Could hear the angels sing.

He spoke to me in dulcet tones,
A twinkle in his heavy-lidded eye,
Words muted by a snuff-stained beard,
Words to behold and to live by,
Words near and yet so far away.

His song, a lullaby,
The same his father sang,
A singsong melody of Hebrew lore,
An old refrain, an invocation,
Shalom for peace, not war.

There were times we slowly walked,
The boy beside the peddler man,
A child entrusted to his care.
We walked, he with his weary steps,
Light-footed, buoyant mine.

We walked, we spoke, his words
Gravely autumnal, mine of sweet spring of youth,
Of goodness, virtue, savants, and fools,
Of sins, punishments, rewards,
Of Jacob wrestling with the angels,
Of paupers, righteous men, and ancient bards.

Then came the years of jackboots,
Of outstretched arm salutes and shouts,
When arbiters of life and death were only men,
And plowshares fashioned into swords again,
And pruning hooks made into spears.

One day we ceased to walk, the peddler man and I,
Uneasy silence, only nods and frightened stares.
When Satan ruled and angels fled,
Good deeds and virtue hid their face,
And brutal slaughter ruled upon in the land.

Then came a day they took the stooped old man,
And while I wept to see him in a cattle train,
Slits windows and the cries for help,
Barbed wires, little hands aflutter to be free,
Black plumes of smoke blotting out the sky.

One day the winds of murder ceased,
The doves of peace returned,
Men, prostrate, genuflecting, swaying once again,
Went on to worship Gods anew, this time the images of men,
But I could only see an empty cattle train,
No Gods to walk with, hand in hand.

The Sand

Some spend their lives collecting gems,
Exotic furs, expensive art, rare stamps,
Or desiccated flowers, wilted leaves
Of gone-by ages, ancient times.

I'm a man of sand,
Gathering the dust of time
From where I came,
To where I must return.

The sand, the grit in one man's eye,
The sandbar, sailor's bane at sea,
The sirocco, the khamsin,
The desert traveler's curse,
A weary traveler's snare,
A nature's deadly sleight of hand.

The rushing river sand,
The soft carpet of the seas,
The building particles of land,
The genesis of dales and hills.

The shifting sands of history,
The burial place of kings and queens,
Of long-forgotten realms
And those obeying their commands.

And while I sift the grains
From hand to hand,
I listen to their whisper
Of long-forgotten lands.

With awe I watch the hourglass,
The flow of sand, the man-made flow of time,
The time clock gauge of birth and death,
The teller when to plow and when to reap.

These are my sands,
These I bequeath to you, my son,
For we are all the dust of time,
The shifting particles of life.

Shana Tova 5761

The clock of eons soon shall chime again.
The hand will move one notch upon the face of time,
And facing east, believers will recite,
"Avinu Malkainu," our Lord sublime.
"Al Khait Khutuni," forgive, absolve
The sinners that we are.

Pardon all misdeeds, transgressions.
Bestow on us and all of our kin
Life, prosperity in the year to come,
As you have done before
To us, the people of your covenant.

So pray for me, my friend,
For on this day of reverence,
This holy day of awe,
Beset by darkness of my doubts,
Doubts born of cold despair,
My lips remain profane.

For I grew deaf,
No longer hear the words of Psalms,
Blind to the ink on parchment scrolls,
Too many died before their time,
Death by the caprice of one's fellow man,
While all the Gods were silent,
Too silent for me to beg, implore.

My Autumn Apple Tree

The winds of a gray autumn
Of melancholy days are near.
The migrant birds have fled.
The earth-born morning mist,
Chilly and inert, fails to lift.
The flowers wilt.

Mourn not, my apple tree,
The bearer of many gifts,
Your leaves turned into butterflies.
Wind-driven, they have come alive
To fly, to land, to rest awhile.
Let's bid them bon voyage
In their autumnal flight.

Weep not, as fluttering they part
In autumn gusts at season's end.
Each tree must let them go
To their retreat, to their repose,
As we must all in time.

'Tis the season, the end of leafy toil,
To join the other butterflies,
Seeking the warm and humid soil,
Season's soft slumber for their wintry night,
A season to dream, to be reborn.

Go stretch your tired limbs,
Shade-giving, fruitful tree.
Unclad, you need your winter sleep
Beneath the eiderdown of snow,
Your branches swaying heavily, and dream,
For soon the balmy winds of spring
Will cause a thousand buds to burst
To greet a newborn sky.

The fragrance of your blooms
Will wake the sleeping bees
Soon to commence their dance,
To sing, to hum, sweet pollen on their wings.
New leaves with sprout, myriad clinging babes,
And you, the mother of them all,
Your limbs, your canopy widespread,
Letting the sun caress their face
Their sustenance their daily bread.

So rest, you arboreal cornucopia,
You legend tree of paradise,
Your trunk the pillow to the dreamer,
Beneath your boughs a lover's tryst,
Your roots the tendril of the earth,
For in the end we all must heed the night
Before we greet the rising sun.

The Clockmaker

In my mind I still can see
The dingy room, my father's shop,
His pride and his domain,
The whitewashed walls, the vast array
Of clocks, small, large, once dutifully
Keeping time, now gone astray.

I see him there, bent over wheels and springs
And softly muttering to none.
He mended things,
The many watches, clocks, the pace of time,
The swinging of a pendulum,
The dulcet chime.

He's gone, the man of broken springs,
The sentinel of time,
Who looked upon me
With a loupe within one eye
And only saw a ticking progeny
In need to mend, to pacify.

A cattle train took him away,
To where so many others went,
Leaving behind his son,
The empty vials of acid and of oil,
The silent clocks upon the wall,
And the forever silenced chimes.

256

The Immigrants

Come, let us cross the stormy sea.
Let us cross as others did before,
Sails lashed by our dreams,
And hope, our rudder and the oar.

No tearful parting from the lands
Where vengeful Gods reside
On crosses, on gilt spires,
On domed temples with a star.

Where lashes were the daily fare
And where the Star of David,
Once pride upon a warrior's shield,
Became the symbol of despair.

Cease gazing at the heaving sea,
The endless undulating span.
Forget the shtetls, hamlets,
Dingy ghettos, huts, the aging clan.

The thatch, the reeking gutters
Along the rutted village lanes,
The clatter of the peasant carts,
The grunting pigs, the braying ass.

Shipwrecked of heart and mind,
The back-bent poor,
And those too proud to stoop,
And those no longer able to endure.

Ill-clad and shivering you stand,
Clutching the salty rail,
Huddled for warmth
Against the autumn gale.

Remember you were former slaves,
As yet not fully freed,
No chains, no fetters, though,
No iron gates.

Your arms tattooed
With numbers, not with hearts,
Your vision limited, confined
By concrete and barbed wire strands.

Come taste the wind, the salty brine
Of freedom yet to come,
A freedom yet deferred,
A dream sublime.

Come now, my shipmates, men of sorrow,
Come, move your tired legs,
Unbend your broken backs.
There is a patch of blue above our heads.

Swing in our hammocks,
Peer into the darkness of the sea,
As yet no castles there,
Only a starry canopy, a heaving sea.

The lady with the torch stands there,
As yet too far away and wrapped in mist.
Like our hopes, she stands at the gate
In tranquil silence, head unbent.

No welcome sign along the shore,
No welcome mat, a steely plank,
An oily concrete ramp,
A dingy hall ahead.

Look, shipmates, at the men in blue and some in gray.
Look at them and soothe your throbbing heart.
You've seen too many men in blue till now,
Too many men with empty stares.

Men, blind to see into your hearts,
To read your thoughts,
Men—only hinges opening the gates
Or closing them once again.

Harsh men and stern,
Men only made to sift, to pry,
Men who forgot their father's blackened face
Of many years gone by.

They gaze without seeing you and want to know
"Yea've somethin' to declare?
Some smuggled goods, some contraband,
Some hanky-panky forgeries, forbidden ware?"

Be silent, tired shipmates,
Don't smile and don't you weep.
He speaks of items to declare—
Your baggage, bundles, duffel bags.

The cherished items lie hidden in your heart,
Invisible, unreadable to all but you.
The time to open them and to declare is years ahead,
When we shall walk like other men
With our heads held high.

To Mourn

For we must mourn them now
Before the rivers of time
Are swallowed by the sea,
Before the chroniclers with crafty pens
Erase that monstrous crime.
Come, let us weep for those whose tears ran dry,
Their voices cast away before their time.

"If I forget thee, O Jerusalem," men wept
Upon a time, bereft of all they lost,
"Let my right hand forget her cunning,
My tongue cleave to the roof of my mouth,"
Their monument, a canticle, a prayer's rhyme,
A dirge, a lament to this day.

We cannot stay the hands of time.
Winds and decay will turn to dust,
An obelisk, a crumbling wall, a lofty monument,
And all the tomes, no matter how sublime
Men will forget, erase, misrepresent.

But while we live, our voices yet undimmed,
Like Rachel weeping for her children,
Let us remember them, for to be silent
Is to join the many, who with diffidence
Watched our children lose their lives
One by one.

Freedom

The ornate gates were sprung, and he was free
To walk away with a wobbly gait,
To wave his spindly arms.
At last he dared to raise his head
To an unblemished summer sky,
To greet the sun, a road ahead,
To let the gentle wind
Caress his ashen face.

And squatting at the river's edge,
He tried to scrub his callous hands.
No soap would cleanse them,
Not even river sands.
None could erase the images
Of pleading, outstretched arms.

The rippling stream was cool,
Bathing his arms, his legs,
Bearing the imprints of his manacles
Of chains upon his flesh,
The whip so painful and so swift,
The curses and abuse
His jailer's parting gift.

Soft, soothing was the shade,
The canopy of summer leaves
Upon his brow
To reverie, to dream of life,
No longer death, the ever-present guest.
But in his dreams before his eyes,
A hangman's noose,

He shackled and undressed,

Free and unbound at last,
Yet wounded was the man,
For these were hurts
Not of the flesh,
Wounds of the soul they were
That none could heal
And only time could help to bear.

Autumn

Time slows to the rhythm
Of soft-falling autumn leaves,
To gently swaying poplar trees,
To my tired, shuffling steps
Through the soft wilt
Beneath my feet.

The morning dew paints silvery
The roadside thistle,
The rolling hills, the river stones,
The half-denuded branches
Of a gnarled apple tree.

My ears attuned to songs of yesterday,
I walk and only faintly hear
The melody of autumn winds.
My tired eyes no longer see
The plumage of the birds in flight.

It is the autumn of the day.
It is the autumn of my life,
My days no longer preludes
Of softly breaking dawns,
Days half-forgotten epilogues,
Adrift white river swans.

Of Nature

I never fail to like a tree,
Its shade, the nesting place for birds,
And when abloom in spring
Of nectar-searching bees
With autumn fruit and heavy boughs,
The fragrant leaves,
A fondling touch upon my face.

I never fail to love a rose in autumn bloom,
Even a wilted one about to shed its leaves
Before its winter sleep,
Their wafting scent carried by the wind,
The autumn-yellowed leaves
A canopy upon the garden bed.

Spellbound, I stand each spring
And watch the irises, their spindly buds,
The pallid, spiky leaves,
The collars and the falls unfold,
A rainbow's gift to lure the eye.

I even like the dandelion,
That wily, sneaky garden weed,
Its pungent yellow bloom, its milky sap,
Wind carried, floating in the air,
A thousand white umbrellas carrying its seed,
To sprout where none would dare.

Oh, yes, I like the flowers and the trees,
And how I wish to say the same
Of Homo sapiens of my creed,
Some of my kin, some neighbor next to me,
Or those who sullenly walk down the street,
Some puffed with pride and full of bigotry.

The Garden

With the hoe in hand,
A song in my breast,
And spring in the air,
I till the fallow soil.
It is my springtime,
My wake-up call for toil.

The springtide morning mist,
Aurora's twilight dawn,
Soft-breaking, almost shy,
Puts the stars to flight,
Caressing the melancholy sky.

The tedious sunless days
Have fled and given way
To sparkling rays.
An avalanche of light rolls down
The mountain slope's incline.

Wan sunshine until now
Is ready to bestow its gifts anew,
The wilted grass upon the hill.
The faded blades of yesterday
Are green again.

There is no crowing of a cock,
No lowing of a cow.
It is the lark, the mockingbird,
To greet the sun,
To swell the pregnant buds,
To let the bees hum once again.

And on such a day of spring,
I till the fallow soil,
With sweat upon my brow,
Creation's legacy upon rebellious man,
His angel with a flaming sword,
Showing the road from paradise to hell.

Defiantly I shake my head,
I swing my hoe and harrow with my rake,
And challenging the angels,
The serpents, and my fate,
I've come back to my garden,
Brandishing my spade,
To live and to reclaim
The sleeping earth again.

Of Sabbath Chants

I hear them sing,
Though their voices have been stilled,
And yet I hear them sing.
The melodies reverberate,
Sweet echoes to this day.

These were the songs,
When I was young,
My chants of yesterday,
The only ones I ever knew.

The solemn hymns
Of slowly swaying men,
Dark twilight entering
The unlit, dingy room.

Recitations in a tired voice
By an old man, and I, his child,
Joining with my lilting tune,
A dream and only half awake.

These were my cradlesongs
Of a long time ago,
My haunting lullabies,
Sorrowful and melancholy,
My reveries and my reality.

Long gone, those chanting men,
The singers swaying back and forth,
Darkly clad, their beards unshorn,
The wide-brimmed hats.

Perished now, forever gone,
But on a Sabbath afternoon
At dusk,
Their plaintive songs still linger on.

To Remember Them

None will remember them.
The tears shed by their sons
In time will cease to flow.
The sorrow finally will end.

The chiseled stones will not withstand
The flaming sun, the burnishing of sand.
The winds will soon erase their names.
Parchments will yellow, crumble.

The thespian's strident voice,
Once droning on the stage,
Will turn to whispers,
Then taper, and then fade.

A children's song,
A fiddler's bow upon a string,
The flicker of a candle,
Then silence—darkness will ensue again.

The hanging gardens of ancient Babylon,
Lighthouses towering upon the sea,
The Mayan temples, ruins now,
Mute witnesses to what they were.

A thousand Gods, those of the sea,
Of fire, and of stone, have come and gone.
Feeble became the scribbler's hand,
His well-honed quill becoming dull.

Vanished now the lecherous king,
Who, with a lyre in his hand,
Sang ruefully his *Shir Hashirim*,
My "Song of Songs."

"Man is like to vanity," he sang,
His days are as a shadow
That passeth away,
His dulcet voice upon a time
Hardly a whisper now.

Reb Shlomo, the Beggar

Welcome, Reb Shlomo,
You mutely stand there at midday,
Stooped, leaning to one side
Like a wind-beaten tree,
Your rugged face, your beard in disarray.

You never smile, Reb Shlomo, never frown.
You enter and silently stand,
Hands hidden in your pockets.
With melancholy eyes you gaze at us,
Without complaint, without reproach.
You never entreat, you never implore.

We know why you are there.
No need for you to speak,
For begging is your trade,
As you proceed from door to door,
Receiving alms, a penny, sometimes more.
You take them as your dues,
Your birthright to receive.

You are no vagabond, Reb Shlomo,
No tramp, no idle derelict, for in your moral code,
To beg is not a vice, to be a beggar no disgrace,
No shame and no dishonor.
To beg is time's respected creed
For us to give our noble deed.

With murmured benediction
On your pale and hardly moving lips,
You settle all your debts, indemnify,
Repay in kind, your words, your blessing,
For pennies, in your outstretched hand,
You look upon as fair exchange.

New Year

Soon the bells will ring.
The silver apple will descend.
Those on the square will cheer,
Blow whistles, clap their hands.
Another year gone by,
A new one is quite near.

Each year the pages of the calendar,
The fallen leaves of time,
Float through the wintry air.
Memento pages of recall,
Once tokens,
Only vestiges and relics now.

Gone are the chronicles,
Gone, the old soggy files
Of yet another year gone by,
When many died in fratricidal wars,
Those worshipping the cross,
Those facing Mecca as they pray.

Gone are the printed images
Of infants, children, tots
With spindly legs, with spindly arms,
Their swollen bellies, vacant stares,
And flailing chests,
Born with a spark of hope, only to die
While groping for their mothers' breasts.

So let us cheer, let us hug, embrace,
As we, well fed, are standing in the square
Or on the ballroom dancing floor,
Gustily chanting the "Auld Lang Syne."
Is it to recall the year that fled?
Or do we cheer, in order to forget?

So let us raise the cup and drink,
Resolving once again to love and to sustain,
To forge the old sword into plowshares,
And into pruning hooks the spears,
As we resolve each year again,
Forgetting that at heart
We are purblind, amnesiac men.

The Enigma Road

The time is near, a decade, two at most,
A tenuous gift of one more year,
To walk the road ahead,
The endless road I trod so long,
The road from where I came,
The road we all must go.

A path we all must walk,
The road an unknown hand had paved for us
When time began, a road without an end,
A road, the journey once began,
Leads to the same mysterious site
From which none has returned to tell.

We walk and walk.
Our footprints, deep or shallow,
Soon shall become obscured
By never-ceasing tides,
Burnished by the sand of time,
No sound, no echoes left.

It was a long and arduous trail,
A glimpse of sunlight
Here and there, a sweet embrace,
The giggle of a child at play,
A sweet whisper in the night,
A frown, a censure, an empty accolade.

Upon a time I walked through storm and gales
That blotted out the sun,
Days of gloom, days of despair,
When raindrops on my face
All had a salty taste
And all my words anathema.

A child, I ran with hurried steps,
To tag, or being tagged,
To chase, or being chased.
As a grown-up man, fatigued by toil,
In quarries or on a cobbler's bench,
I trotted tiredly and spent.

And on that lifelong endless trek,
I glimpsed at those I left behind
And those who passed and those ahead,
And those who tarried for a while,
And those I led to a canopy to wed,
And those I followed to their end and wept.

And now I walked the road all men must take,
As often as I raised my eyes
To read the signpost written in the sky,
One arrow there, none pointing back,
Another pointing way ahead.
"Enigma," each one said.

Perfection

How would I know
The perfect harmony of sound
Without a false note in a song's refrain,
Enjoy an apple's autumn blush
Without a wormhole or a stain?

A maiden's blush without a blemish
Is all too perfect to be real.
The perfect stillness of a forest night,
Save for the flutter of a frightened wing,
The footsteps of an animal in flight.

The turquoise velvet of a summer sky,
Without a leaden rainy day,
In time turns tedious to the eye,
The stillness of a pond
Without the rushing of a stream.

And so it is with my beloved.
How would I comprehend her soft caress,
Her kisses, and her smile
Without a sometime lament or a tear,
A silly spat once in a while?

My Rose

Come, come, bare-bottom child of mine,
Your spindly, thorny arms
Mere twigs stretched out to be embraced.
Disrobed, you're asking to be swaddled,
Kept warm, kept damp,
Your roots, myriad hungry mouths
To suckle the moist ground.

"Each morn, a thousand roses bring …"
Omar, the ancient poet, sang,
And humbly do I ask
For you to be my only one,
At dawn to grace my garden bed,
White as the freshly fallen snow,
Or sanguine red.

Your petals pink, the edges red,
A maiden's courtship blush,
You stretch your limbs
To greet the summer sky.
For every rose there is a painful thorn,
The sages claim, but I deny.
To me your scent atones for being stung.

Weep not. At season's end
You too must fade,
As we must all in time,
But until then bestow your charm,
Your hues, your sweet incense,
Sweet maiden of my garden realm.

My Valentine

It's cold, the sky,
A panhandler's, pauper's,
Windswept and forlorn,
Wanting and lost.

And then soft sounds reach my ear—
A murmur, a faint melody,
An old refrain I hear,
The pain has gone, my heart can beat again.

I recognize it now,
For it was you, my love.
You never left.
You always stood there at my side.
My vision only dimmed for a short while.

Unseen you were,
Unseen yet there,
To touch with an unseen heart.
Spouse, comrade, wife—
Take any other name you want—
To me, you are my life.

The End Was Near

Suddenly the clock struck hard,
Vanished, gone the dulcet chime,
Dividing night from day,
The throbbing clock to herald once again
The morning glow.

The chime struck hard,
And in that deadly knell
My vision dimmed,
And suddenly a gloomy dusk
Eclipsed the midday sun
And day gave way to night.

The wheels of time began to slow,
The gears no longer meshed.
They slowed but didn't cease to turn.
They mustn't stop, not yet, not yet,
Moving my lips, I whispered to myself.

I couldn't see but knew
That all the rivers ceased to flow.
The roads ahead of me
Had reached their end.
Here stood the sign: "Nothing Beyond."

Not yet, not yet, I wished to say
With a pain constricted throat
And mutely moved my lips,
A beggar begging for another day,
A grant, an offering, a gift.

Then stillness all around me,
Cold, chilling,
Bleak, solemn,
An utter silence only I could hear,
Forbidding, sinister, and grim.

A spark lit somewhere,
A soft whisper far away,
The fluttering of lips
Of other men, not mine,
Staring at the glassy screen with knitted brows.

And from my ebbing pain,
I rose to greet another day,
And stillness of the night
Gave rise to a soft tune
Of rippling waves.
The river flowed again.

They spoke, the men in scrub suit blue,
A whisper, hushed, an undertone,
"Look, look, it beats again, his heart,
A rhythm, and extra beat, a sigh."
Their solemn chat rings in my empty ears.
They spoke of life, not death.

And still unsure whose life was on the scale,
Light flooded the darkened stage.
The pain abated and I perceived
That life grew wings.
It was my life, the whisperer's refrain.

It was my life and I was home again.
The thistles in my heart
Gave way to lips,
Soft, roseate upon my sweaty brow,
For she was there beside me—
Her seal, her affirmation, and her vow.

Memories

I can no longer recollect the names
Of towns, those of my many friends,
The labor in the quarries on scorching summer days,
The numbing chill, my frozen hands, the icy rails,
The gnawing hunger, the jailer's lash, the many ills.

My memory, a coarse-meshed sieve
Of hate abroad, curses, maledictions,
The coarse, striped cloth, the misty rain,
An emblem on my chest,
A number for my name.

Gone are the many women, men,
The good, the evil ones,
The many who I cherished once,
The fragrance of a lilac sprig,
Or was it just the soft caress,
A loving woman's hand?

There is one day beyond erase,
A day, an ancient obelisk
Impervious to the ravages of times,
The way we stood there,
Thousands with bundles at our feet.

But to my eyes she was the only one,
A child, a daughter, a mother,
Clutching hands,
Mine clutching hers convulsively,
She gently pushing me away.

With downcast gaze,
A stifled whisper,
An echo of a sob, she was telling me
The time had come for us to part,
To part, perhaps to never meet again.

That I, her son,
Her only child, must run
While there was time
Before the gate was closed beyond recall,
But she, bound by a filial duty of her own,
She could not go, she must remain.

I still recall her trembling hand,
Our downcast eyes to hide our tears.
If clasping hands could speak
And racing hearts could scream,
These were the loudest farewells.
None can erase that day.

Tattoos

We bear tattoos on our arms,
So many more in our hearts,
Blue inked, indelible, beyond erase,
For all to see, a sore to our tired eyes.

We've learned to grieve in silence,
Bear our wounds with consternation.
And when we speak, be it in prose or verse,
We hide them from the fickle light of day,
From comments, innuendos, callousness, ill will.

And though we hope and wish
For our wounds to heal,
And like the sky at dusk
Their blue to fade, each number
Takes to wings and flees unseen
And yet tenaciously they cling, they stay.

The Conch

I found a conch upon the shore,
Half-buried in the sand,
Pink, salt-crusted, pitted,
Buffeted, tossed by the ebb
And by the flowing tide,
Gently swaying to and fro,
Bidding me to pick it up,
To set it free, to let it go.

I placed it to my ear
And listened to its whisper.
"Come to the sea, far, far away,
Where no one dared to venture yet,"
It spoke to me
In singsong of the sand and sea.

"Come where the windswept, sparkling waves
Mirror the sun in multicolored hues,
Pellucid, sky-hued, emerald at noon.
At night the lustrous moon
Spreads silver on the surf,
And all is calm and all serene.

Sanguine though and dark at times,
The sea thunders angrily; it roars
At the buffeting and leaden sky,
Heaving, whirling, white-crested,
A dancing dervish, a drunken tar.

Playful and tumbling at other times,
A puppy dog, a newborn colt,
A child in the meadows at springtime,
Dancing, twisting, a young lion
Tossing his mane, pawing at the sky.

But down below the water's skin,
Life throbs in its deep-bosomed realm,
Life, agreeable, plankton-laden,
Primordial life, the womb of all that is alive today,
The cradle of all things on foot or in the air,
Even of you, you curious man.

Deep down, unseen to you
The smiling dolphins play,
And shoals of silver fish
Like ballerinas dance
The stingrays flap their angel wings,
The crawling starfish,
Stars fallen from the sky.

Are you still listening, old man?
Just nod your head.
I've told my tale so many times,
The designated spokesman of the sea.
I am verbose, long-winded;
I ramble on and on
Like an aged actor, like an old ham.

I feel the trembling of your hand
And sense the frowning of your brow.
What is the glamour of the sea? you ask,
Half-spoken like a man.
You shake your head.
I do detect a smirk upon your face.

What is the virtue living there? you wish to know.
You upright-walking, bipedal man
Who built the pyramids,
Exploded atom bombs,
Flew faster than the speed of sound,
Claimed to be master of us all.

Well, let me whisper it to you
In my conch idiom of the sea.
There is no bondage there, no slavery.
There are no killing fields, no Holocaust,
For man has never lived beneath the waves.

And so you see, old man,
Down at the bottom of the sea,
The graveyard of your detritus,
Your ships, a sailor's last ahoy,
The many plundered treasure troves,
And yet, in spite of it, all this
Is freedom land, my dear."

Deliverance

We are free now,
Unfettered and unshackled,
Free as the wind,
Capriciously unbound
To tilt the sails,
To turn the windmill wings.

Free as the swallows
To choose the eaves,
To build their nests in spring,
The warbler picks its branch
To sing amid the leaves.

We are free now,
Though we dare not look behind,
For each one casts
A shadow of his past,
The remnants of his yoke
Of whom he was.

Of Things Ephemeral

The miracles of life,
Walt Whitman's *Leaves of Grass*,
The mockingbird, its song,
The apes to Jane Goodall,
To us, our God,
To God, the universe at large.

The newborn child,
Blessed in its innocence,
The toothless smile, the grasping hand,
The cooing in its crib, its song,
Its first poetic utterances at dawn.

The crystal spring that gushes from a rock,
Earth's gift to quench the thirsty man,
The spider clinging to the moss,
The emperor penguin, the egg between his toes,
Braving the arctic storm.

The eager groom, the blushing bride,
The sigh, the language of the night,
The sound, the touch,
The spark, a lightning bolt,
Invisibly begetting man.

To soothe his ignorance, his fears,
Combating monsters in his sleep—
Man coined it miracle of life.
Is it a miracle indeed,
Or is it only make-believe?

Abstractions, concepts, esoteric laws,
The endlessness of space, of time,
Eternity, without beginning, without end,
A sham they are, a self-deceptive lie.
For eons hence the end will come
By stealth, by frost, by fire from the sky.

The flaming star above will burst,
The earth, a barren comet aimlessly adrift,
And man-made God, that sallow-bearded man
With so much sorrow in his face,
With death of man, God too will die.

The Echo of the Past

Beyond the seven mountains and the seven seas,
Beyond Sambation, the Rubicon, and Styx,
The sounds of my life had come to a halt.
The terminus, the final stop, the end
Of my allotted time between then and now.

Here stands the sentinel,
Winged brother to the man at Eden's gate.
"No trespassing," says the flaming sign,
But if you wish to hear
Your life resound again,
Turn back. The echoes of your past
Are in the shadows and quite near.

And like the albatross around your neck,
Your past is there, unseen to none but you,
The past all men must learn to bear.
It is their deadweight,
A refuge or a blessing,
To some a sad anathema.

"Beware the past," the winged man spoke,
"For in your retrospective journey there
Are other gates, inviting some.
They lead to paradise,
Some lead to hell,
Most to the quicksand of your mind."

I turn at my shadow and nod consent
At my companions of the past,
And hear the muted ticking of a clock.
The sounds I thought had ceased
Obediently came back,
Scraping and bowing,
Elbowing each other,
Anxious to be first.

I hear an infant cry,
His mother's first,
The rustling of a shirt,
The softness of the breast, a lullaby,
A couplet with the infant's cooing.
"I wed thee"—words upon a time,
Now only shards.

A murky study room,
A splintered wooden bench,
The teacher dozing off, asleep,
And I, the student, diffident, averse,
Recite unwillingly in half-song
Black dots, the alphabet of long ago.

And then I sing
The circle, round and round,
Feet stomping on the dusty floor,
Thanking the Lord for the sun, the sky,
The restless feet allowed to chase
A yellow butterfly,
To run with a dog, to kick a soggy ball.

Striped men and sunken eyes,
A bowl in hand, we stand in line,
Stooped backs and shuffling feet.
And walking to the fence
I see a friend of mine
About to touch the wire strands.
No, no. I turn my face. No longer can I gaze,
Too long my shadow, too much, too much.
I wish my shadow farewell, good-bye.

The River

Light-footed, half carried aloft by the wind,
I ran along the trodden path,
My running mate, the river down below,
Only a brook, but to my eye
A mighty river then.

The melting snow, the springtime rains,
My river tumbles, ocher, muddy,
Whipped by a gauntlet of overhanging boughs.
Full of anger, it roars.
Rushing, it spills its banks
To reach the tranquil comfort of the sea.

Craving for the past,
I have returned to visit my old friend,
My former running mate.
I was a boy then;
Now I am a stooped old man,
Resting my arms on the bridge's wooden rail.

I gaze with longing eye
At what was once my river down below,
A muddy brook, a rivulet, a trickle now—
Oil-sleeked, weed-overgrown, the current slow.
With hesitating steps I reach the edge.
Gone are the pollywogs, the croaking toads.
Only a stillness now remains.

Was there a river many years ago?
The barking of a mongrel dog,
The milkman's wagon clattering
Along the cobbled street at dawn,
A bearded man in gabardine,
Walking, a cane to pace his gait.

Was ever there a boy with racing feet,
Daring the river of his youth, daring the wind,
Or is it just an old man's dream,
A silent dirge for things that were
And now forever gone?

The Blue Jay

Come, blue Jay, do not fear.
Come closer, as you come each day
To shake your crested head at me,
Your song a rattling of an empty can,
You beggar screeching for some alms.
And with distrust you then procure,
And without thanks you dart away.

With feathers for a diadem,
The way you strut
Along my humble windowsill,
The way you always preen,
The way you screech,
You certainly must be an avian queen.

I do not know your name,
You stranger on the piney bough,
Nor do you know who I might be.
It doesn't matter, beggar friend,
We know each other just the same.
You are a bird, I am a man;
The bread crumbs are for you to claim.

To Remember Them

We are the fallen leaves,
The mold, the detritus of life,
Discarded, youth never to return,
And yet we still are there
In dog-eared sepia photographs,
Remembered in a song.

We are the stooped beneath the peddler's bag,
Shopkeepers standing on the threshold of his store
And murmuring with sullen stares,
An invitation to come in to buy
Or just to look at our wares.

The men behind the butcher's block,
The pushcart men, their pleading voice,
The cobblers, smithies, handymen,
Once architects of pyramids, now only of adobe huts,
Beating the cadences of our toil with quill and pen.

Slaves once, then masters, and then slaves again,
The makers of a rich man's furs,
And diadems to crown the kings
And for the poor
The patches on their pants.

Although our backs are bent,
Our beards are gray,
We still discuss, debate,
And circumnavigate
The words of our sages,
The wisdom of the yesterdays.

Though you've watched and wept,
Seeing us squatting in a marketplace
And then boarding trains, never to be seen again,
Was it only an illusion,
A sleight of hand of the Almighty,
Or a bad dream?

As long as we recall
The cobblestones on which we trod,
The musty odor of the narrow lanes,
And while we still can hear the plaintive songs
Of swaying, bearded men,
Beseeching on a Sabbath day,
We will remember them.

The Morning Mist

The fog lifts
At dawn,
A fisherman's net,
Drenched and waterlogged,
Drawn by the cold and stubby fingers
Of men tending the sea.

A milky coat
Sprayed on my windowpanes.
Far off, I hear the singing
Of a mockingbird,
The tuning of a fiddle,
Before the melody begins.

The foghorn's plaintive song,
Only a lilting mantra hum,
Doors slam, dogs bark,
The garbage can a brassy drum,
A jogger's slapping footsteps.

New tunes are there
To wake the day,
The men behind the wheels
Revving their cars
A euphony to modern ears,
Shattering the mystery of night.

The dawn cast off the morning veil,
A spray of sun has lit the poplar trees,
Soft swaying candles
On the altar of another day,
The hills dark painted until now,
No longer ashen gray,
Are now aglow.

I've cast my dreams aside,
Dew-scented light
Erased my nightly apparitions.
The mist of night
Has given way to day.
The clock has chimed again.

Look Up

Look up, my children,
Look, the stars are there,
Erased each day
By solar light,
A sponge against
The azure tablet
To tell us day
From night.

Look up, my children,
The stars are there,
As yet unseen
But have no fear,
The sun will set,
The clouds will part,
The fog will clear,
And you will
See them once again.

Look up and see
A broken necklace string,
And million pearls strewn
Upon the canopy of night—
No broom to sweep them up
No hands to gather them,
To string them once again.

Look, can you see
The great Orion,
The Northern Polar star,
The Milky Way,
The blushing planet Mars,
The faithful guardians
Of the men at sea?
They twinkle with a lullaby
For us to dream.

Remember

Look down upon the ground,
You *Herrenvolk*, and shed a tear.
The footprints of your past are there,
Embedded in eternal stone,
Etched into the skin of the earth,
Cut with a whip into the solid crust,
The never-healing welts upon the backs
Of those you have enslaved.

Look there, the imprints
Of the many walking men,
Millions of feet, some large,
Some small, a child, a woman,
The young, the lame, the very old,
Reluctant children dragging tired feet.

And over there a tattered shoe,
A wooden clog, a prison cap,
An imprint of a hand
Of those who begged
To be allowed to live another day,
While trudging to an unmarked grave.

Look at those footprints
Up and down your roads.
They are the wormholes of your land,
Of you who gazed at the heavens
In search of long-forgotten Gods
And bleated like so many sheep,
Ein Volk, ein Reich, ein Fuehrer,
Look now and weep.

The Garden of Eden

Come, you sons of Abraham,
Cease longing for the lands you've left.
It was no earthly paradise;
It was an earthly hell.

Polluted, weed-infested land of bitter fruits,
Where even roses had a putrid smell,
And the inhabitants,
Blond, blue-eyed serpents,
Your pugilistic friends.

You were expelled for daring to partake
Of wisdom and of lore.
You have transgressed
Beyond redemption.
You've sinned beyond amends.

And in that other paradise,
You and your branded sons
Were shown the exit gate,
As you've been shown since then,
Unwelcome you were there
And everywhere you went
Since dawn of men.

Wilted now, the gardens of your Babylon,
Jerusalem, a vale of tears,
Saintly kings, wise prophets,
Men of prose and song,
Of parchments and of scrolls,
The temples, scattered stones,
Lay ruined at your feet.

The dulcet notes of your Espania,
Discordant music to your ears,
Flames, chanting hooded monks,
The ringing bells that tolled
Of holiness and death
Under the shadow of the cross.

Once venerated Schiller, Goethe, Kant—
Their pugilistic sons exchanged
The quills for hobnailed boots and guns,
No longer *Liebeslieder*,
No longer dulcet tunes, cantatas, chants,
Their songs a chilling hymn to death.

And you, the worshippers of one and only God,
The chosen ones, the shining light
That blinded other men
And branded you the outcasts of their realms,
Are you still craving for the past?
Must you be shown the door again?

The Flight

Run, run, my kinsman.
Run, do not turn to gaze,
And do not grieve
With teary eye
Over the conflagration of your life.

Do not look back.
Run, run in haste.
Nostalgia for the past
Is nothing but a waste
To sap your strength.

You're not the first.
How many times from distant shores
Your father and their fathers fled,
Their voices muted echoes now,
Their tears, sap of their wounded souls.

Reaching the sea, tumbled by the sand,
Tears turned to amber,
Each one another bead
In the long necklace of your past,
Another exile to recall.

A Reminder

I write, my hand,
A drunkard's midnight stride.
My letters reel from side to side,
And yet I write,
Compelled to speak,
To break the silence
Of a heartbreak night,

So let the written word
Become a sleight of hand,
An act of magic
To conjure up the past

No arias there,
A simple melody,
A mumbled song,
A wordless hum.

Each phrase a signpost,
A reminder who I was
Not long ago,
And who I am,
Or think I am, today.

Free at Last

Free at last, like the blushing leaf,
Free to spread my wings and soar,
The autumn-gilded butterfly
Carried aloft by the updrafts of the air,
No longer do I need to flap my wings.

I'm free to wade through mounds
Of fallen autumn leaves
And listen to the whispers
Of wind-stirred branches,
My full orchestral score.

My pebbly garden path to walk along,
The Eden of my waning years,
Hands in my pockets,
Merrily tapping my foot
In rhyme to a warbler's song.

Unshackled, freed from days
Of wooden clogs and prison garb,
I praise the sky, the golden hills,
The lichen-painted stones,
The music of a nearby child at play.

I must no longer scrape
Or bow, or bend my aching back
To please. No longer must I weep.
No longer do I thirst
Nor yearn for food.

I'm free at last and do not care
If others frown at all my sins,
No longer placate idols of the past.
Gone is the awe, the heedless worship
Of my capricious Gods.

At last I bask in full recollection
The many moments of the past.
I'm the never-sated hummingbird,
Though tired are my wings.
The sunset near, I'm satisfied at last.

The Mist on the Hill

The red-tailed hawk is on the wing
To ride the up-drift of the air.
The foghorns on the bay,
Base fiddlers of the night,
No longer moan their plaintive cries.

The dusky hills are lit again;
I fix my gaze upon them
With drowsy, morning eyes.
My limbs astir again,
I bid adieu the night.

The misty curtain's lacy hem
Has reached the dusky sky.
A eucalyptus tree along the crest
Began its morning sway
To greet the sun, its morning guest.

The climbing sun
Has set aflame the wind-caressed
And sun-bleached oats,
The Scotch broom, yellow mustard.
Gnarled clumps of oaks
Have cast their shadows on the ground.

I've come to greet the light,
One man's call to joy,
Remembering the days
When darkness fell upon my eyes,
And unlike then, I gaze and smile.

Two does, Aurora's children
Enter from the misty shade
To greet another day,
A day for them—
The day is also mine.

The Garden in May

My bride, the month of May,
My canopy, the branches of my apple tree—
I am the groom.
It is my garden's wedding day.

No winter chill, no frost,
But petal snowflakes—
A shower of confetti
Land on my nuptial garb,
My garden apparel, my jaunty hat.

Daylilies, Irish bluebells,
The wedding flowers at my feet,
The revelers, the nectar-drinking,
Base-fiddling bumblebees
Reeling from cup to flower cup,
Already drunk in ecstasy

The blue jays are my wedding guests.
The larks, pedestrian sparrows,
The merry-making mockingbirds,
My music makers for the day,
Are here to serenade.

And in their song I hear
The preacher's wedding words:
"To everything there is a season,
There is a time to plant, a time to reap.
A time to bloom, a time to fruit."

"Let it be," I hear a whisper in the wind.
"Let it be," nods the bud-heavy bough.
The sun has reached the hidden crest,
Setting my revelers aglow,
And as I listen with enchanted ear,
I sing along, "Oh, yes, so let it be,
So let it be, my dear."

Dreams

Defiant of the sandman's rule,
Some never dream,
But I, attuned to the flutter
Of a night owl's wing,
Am lulled to sleep,
And, having fled reality, embrace pretense.
Dissolve the real me.

When dusk becomes the gate to dream,
I vanish from myself,
Plunge into a nonexistent realm
Where only darkness looms
Without beginning, without end.
When time is shown the door,
The clock turns mute.
The pendulum has ceased to swing.

And in that flight of fantasy,
Self-exiled, being all alone,
Concealed from man-made storms
And from abysmal ruin,
I find repose and solitude,
A place where man-made storms
No longer rage.

I am afraid to tell my dreams,
A travesty, a mockery,
Anathema to some,
A discord minor sound,
A dissonance to many ears.

A stream of light, my wake-up call,
I hear the ticking of a clock,
And know it was a lie, a fanciful illusion,
The quenching of a thirst, a moment's flight.
I am alive to greet the day.
The next-door children sing again.

Home, Sweet Home

My native land, my home,
The land of dreamers and their dreams,
Hills, marshes, sandy shores,
The cold and windy Baltic Sea,
And long-abandoned castles on its hills,
Hooded monks and black-robed priests,
The strutting officers in shining boots.

The black Madonna on the hill,
White roses clutching to her heart,
The gilded altars lit by candlelight,
Hands folded, breviaries, and rosaries,
Black shawls, bent heads,
Kneeling in prayer, mumbling men.

There stood the old adobe hut,
The fading whitewashed paint,
The thatch, rain barrels under eaves,
The ever-present mold, the soot
A dingy room, the earthen floor.
Here I was born; here my cradle stood.

Back alleys, rutted paths,
The heat of summer dust, the autumn mud,
The wintry flurries, the frozen pond,
My father's shouts in anger, some in jest,
His songs, his speech, my lullabies—
This was my shelter; this was my nest.

I was a barefoot boy, daring the wind,
Kicking the boy-made dust,
The roadside ditch, a brook, a little stream,
The stinging nettle weeds,
The shadow of my apple tree,
A place to dream.

A rooster's heralding the dawn,
My morning wake-up call,
A summon to another day,
The schoolboy walking with his shuffling feet,
A dingy room, a splintered wooden bench,
And singsong recitation of an ancient text.

Midsummer light, black shadows in the dust,
The heat of day, the chill at night,
The mud-streaked banks of melting snow,
The icicles upon the eaves,
The flight of bats across the purple sky,
The naked trees, another year gone by.

My land of sun-bleached barns,
Familiar faces, forgotten now,
Though some I still recall—
Gaunt, weather-beaten, and begrimed,
The young, the old, the haggard,
Those full of hope, those long resigned.

Once they were there, the bearded old,
The young grown old before their time,
Yakovs, Yossefs, Solomons,
The pushcart peddlers, traders,
Toilers toting bundles on their backs,
So many stooped beneath
The burden of their lives.

They've gone; they are no more,
But I, with bow upon my cello's strings,
I hear the Klezmer flute, base fiddle, drums,
The sound of dancing feet,
And on a Sabbath afternoon I hear them sing.
I see them nod and sway.
Bereaved I wish they were still there.

The Mystery of Time

Speak to me, dear physicist,
Of particles that swirl with speed of light,
Of apogees, trajectories,
Those that you so cleverly scan,
Who fashioned them, the protons, electrons,
And placed them all alight.

Who pushed the cosmic pendulum to swing,
Placed numbers on the face of clocks,
Then fashioned men, enchanted by their ring,
Men who would name the flow of time,
Men who could fly, could walk, could swim?

Who created earth's gravity
For men to walk, for butterflies to fly,
The blossoms on a branch each spring,
The water rushing down a brook,
The doves and falcons on the wing?

Who set the moon to spin around the earth,
To be for us the lunar date, the monthly score,
The hand that hurled the earth to spin
Around the sun, then set ablaze its core?

Who struck the first percussion wave
Against the drum of our curious human ears,
For us to hear and to perceive the sound,
The rods, the cones, the lens in our eyes?

Unfold those mysteries of time, dear physics man.
Who created infinity of space and why?
Who cast the light upon the sea
So we may fathom when it all began
And when the end might come?

Old Man Levko

Old Levko was his name, a tiller of the soil,
Clasping the handles of his plow,
Gnarled fingers, weather-beaten face,
The gleaming blade, the prow,
Cleaving the earthen waves,
Churning a stubble-covered row.

Whoa! I still can hear his shout,
The swishing of his whip
Upon the straining nag, its hollow back,
The yoke, the bit, the foamy sweat,
Black ravens swooping down
To feast upon the upturned row.

In times of plenty, of abundant crests of golden wheat,
Old Levko was content. He was the sovereign
Over his land, his hut, his children, and his wife,
But there were other days, stark famine days
Of barren fields, of stunted sheaves, of hungry eyes.
An evil eye had struck, and Levko cursed.

And so he labored on his land,
With plow and harrow, sickle, and his scythe,
The soil, his flesh, his blood,
Stooped, bent—I see him now,
Shielding his eyes against the glaring sky,
Wiping his face, his tired brow.

Well, I recall the squeaking wheel,
The water splashing back into the well,
The village church, the Sunday morning bell,
The gilded dome, the double-transom cross,
The scented air, the pew,
The singing of a hymn.

Empty the church, the villagers have left,
The bearded priest, the acolytes have gone,
Old Levko in his pew, the only one,
No longer can he hear, no longer see,
And none to recall his name.

The Winds of Time

Be kind, be gentle, eternal winds of time.
Let the few maple leaves still flutter on the bough
Before they turn to autumn brown,
And seeking shelter on the ground,
Become the wintry eiderdown.

Be gentle with the shuffling man,
Round-shouldered, weighted down
By burdens long beyond recall,
Once keeper of the gate and now unknown.
Be gentle in his autumn years.

And let him dream a while.
Give him your gifts, your alms.
To him, whose past
And present have become but one,
Be gentle with the shuffling man.

Dreamers

Your dreams, your playmates of the night,
Descend upon you
In silent shoes like thieves,
The moonlight casting silver halos
On softly swaying drapes.

I see a smile across your musing lips.
Sleep well, my mate, the sandman sings
Your nightly lullaby.
You nod your head, you sigh,
The curtains softly sway.

At times, my dreams
Do enter with a thud,
A herd of horses at full gallop
With thunder, foam-lipped, all unshod,
While grim-faced riders urge them on.

An avalanche of shouts,
Of languages I once have known,
Pale, misty phantoms,
Enigmas, mystifying, a cracked mirror,
A forgery, a mockery of who I am
Or who someday I might become.

Late Autumn Days

Long past the harvest days,
The wintry cold
Comes creeping in by stealth.
The morning dew turns into rime
And hoarfrost blankets,
The brown-spotted stubble
Of past summer rye.

Before the hush of night,
His trembling hand
Clutches the old gnarled cane,
Once his companion,
Waiting to be used again,
The cane his father braced
In his own autumn time.

Silent the hut now,
Silent the treadle, the spinning wheel,
The mournful, plaintive songs—
No infant squall, no sullen discontent,
His sons, one gone to war, never to return,
A scoffer, Antichrist the other,
A daughter, errant and forlorn.

He leaves the hut, the bearer of the cane,
Tall once, no longer need to bend,
Beneath the lintel of the door,
The rusty hinges, the timeworn stoop,
The whitewashed crumbling walls.

Wearily he walks, the stooped old man,
For out there bids the leaf-strewn path,
Softly to cushion his stride.
The yellow leaves too had come to rest,
Their summer days unspent.

He walks with swaying stride,
The night, the season of the parting,
Between the being and the dream,
Stark and eternal,
Awaits the night without a dawn,
And there ahead, in still anticipation,
A bench hewn from a log.

Shaped by his father,
It stands beneath the branch
At the pond's edge,
A place to rest, to dream,
Like many others who came here,
Summoned by the night without a day.

I Only See Myself

How often have I walked
The cobbled streets,
The crumbling, littered sidewalks,
Stepped over putrid gutters,
My eyes upon my weary feet,
But rarely saw many
Squat against the crumbling walls,
Their hungry eyes, the wistful gaze,
The sunken cheeks.
Though I caught sight of them,
I only saw myself.

And in the days of famine,
How often have I walked
The twisting country lanes,
Along a split rail, weather-beaten fence,
The barren fields,
The rusty, long-abandoned plows,
The gaunt and raw-boned nags,
The stubble-searching cows,
The many stooped with hoe in hand,
But only saw myself.

In terror-stricken days,
I ran to save my life.
Fear-stricken and with pounding heart,
I ran, oblivious to so many others
In our headless flight
And overcome by horror
And by a paralyzing fright.
I only saw myself.

And later on, while searching for a better land,
The wings of peace my sails,
Horizons still far off,
I and my shipmates
Gazed upon the parting waves.
We gazed and dreamed,
And even then
I only sought salvation of myself.

And even now,
About to ebb their flow,
With failing sight and muted sound,
I gaze upon the mirror of the past,
Abashed by what had been.
I try to see what lies ahead,
Beyond the curtain of the known,
And still, I only see myself.

A Plea to Erato

If I could use only my words,
Each one a scented petal of a rose,
Mellifluous and without barbs,
Devoid of wilt and slow decay.

Words to console, not vilify,
Poignant, without prattle,
To be whispered, not shouted,
Lilting words, not harsh,
Conveying passion.

Words flowing, rushing,
Like a mountain spring,
Each one a sonnet,
"Scheherazade," recite and sing
To calm her sultan's ire.

Teach me to use a simple phrase,
Iambic pentameters,
Or plain blank verse,
A limerick, a nurse's rhyme,
My pen a master's brush
To soothe the weary eye.

Now in the season of denuded boughs
And wilting leaves of yesterday,
So much already has been lost
In sorrow and dismay.
Let me not lose my words;
Just let them be mine and stay.

Silence

Hush now, let silence reign
Along the empty streets,
Where children hopped and skipped,
And lovers, arms entwined,
Went on their sunset stroll,
And bearded men walked on and on.

Hush now, let silence reign
Over an old man's chant,
The laughter of a child,
A mother's frantic call.

Hush now, the silent homes,
The windows with their broken panes
Stare soullessly like blinded men,
Each home, each hut a solemn tomb.

Only a brooding echo
Within the rooms of broken doors,
Of unmade beds, of empty cribs,
Of silent clocks upon the wall.

Hush now, the silence of a town,
Not of repose, it is the silence of demise,
Of broken songs,
Each one a dirge of things now gone.

Gone is the songstress of a lullaby.
Gone are the children in her arms.
Gone are the medleys, the last children's cry,
Gone, never to return.

Silently I beg, no more, never again,
The sound of hobnailed boots,
The rumbling of a distant train,
The clanking of a gun, the rattling of a chain.

Hush now, my fellow man,
Let tearful silence reign.

The Homeless

I see you, fellow homeless man,
Squatting on the sidewalk.
Wordlessly you beg with bloodshot eyes.
Is it a piece of bread you crave?
Is it the balm to soothe your pain?

You squat, you stand with unkempt beard,
Unwashed and clad in tattered pants,
The ever-present cardboard sign your calling card,
Clasped in your weather-beaten hands.

I know you well,
For once upon a time,
I too used doorways, stoops, a soggy bench.
Like you, I sought a glance, an affirmation
That I was man, like other men.

And sheltered for the many days,
And sheltered for the many nights,
Cold shelters were my realm,
My vision, my horizons,
Rows upon rows of man-made thorns.

I dare not meet your gaze,
For once, bereft of home,
I also knew compassion's stingy hand.
Because of faith or color of our skin,
We were despised by fellow men.

Today I walk along the well-paved streets,
Halt at the many crosswalk lights,
My springy steps, my patent shoes,
Soft leather gloves,
Well groomed and satisfied.

I swerve; I shun your gaze,
A wound that never healed,
And giving haste to my quick stride,
I dare not run, and yet I wish
To be far from where I've come.

With eyes averted
And with trembling hand,
I reach for a coin—no, not a coin,
Only a token for a wishful breach
Between my past and now.

Farewell to My Prison Clogs

Let me embrace you one more time,
As you embraced my blistered heels,
My soles, half-frozen toes,
On days of ice,
Nocturnal mates of weary rest,
Forced marches, tramping in a prison yard,
The pillows for my tired head,
And dreams of open skies and fragrant moss.

You had been there to soothe my head
When searchlight-splintered starlit skies;
A sandman moon hung limply
Between the wire strands.

Each day we marched to toil
The deathly quarry, the sandy, rocky ground.
Clip-clop you sang along with other clogs,
A prisoner's beating heart, our song.

Farewell, my clogs, sabots, clodhoppers,
The Sabbath of the toil arrived at last.
Your splintered soles, the worn-down heels,
Ask for a respite, as does my heart, as does my soul.

Rest in the attic of my unwanted dreams,
And gather dust, the dust of peace.
Go rest and let us hope no man to ever wear
The prison clogs or hobnailed boots.

Some claim that we may meet again,
Old comrade of so many years ago,
And in that realm of dust to dust,
My dust and yours be one.

A Love Poem

Two scores and ten,
I drew your face with trembling hand
Upon a canvas of my mind,
My signature, an oath,
A ring, a wedding band.

Each day I look upon it,
It is still there,
The wistful gaze,
The same soft eyes—
They haven't changed.

No wintry blight
Erased that countenance,
My vision still undimmed.
I see it now.

Your voice, more mellow to my ear
And yet I crave to hear
The songs you sang so softly
A day ago, a week, a year.

The canvas drawn upon,
A precious mirror now
Of every day, and every night
I look at it and see you there.

I Can Hear

Lulled by encroaching silence
Of a lifelong span of time,
I still can hear the sweet harmony
Of pebbles gliding in the tide,
Their E-flat pebble song
In contrapuntal ripple of the waves.

I can hear the children sing
"Humpty Dumpty,"
"Ring Around the Rosie,"
The cries, the laughter,
The chiming of their little bells,
The atonality of their songs.

I can hear the brassy drone
Of black-winged bumblebees,
Base fiddle player's monophonic hum,
And those aloft, the mockingbirds,
The mimes, the mimics,
The thieves of avian songs.

The polyphonic rasping
Of door hinges,
The barefoot steps at night,
The creaking of a floorboard,
The whisper in an upbeat duo,
The all-embracing sigh.

And in the silent cold,
A midnight hidden moon,
I hear the soft drumming,
A gust of an April breeze.
I sigh with long-remembered joy
Of wishful nights.

And so with tired ears,
I silently lip-read
The melodies, the bridal songs,
Bells, prayers, weeping fiddlers on the roof,
The sunrise, the vespers,
The plainsongs of many days ago.

The Last Applause

It could have been a comedy
Or just an agonizing drama.
The play has ended,
As it once began.

And with the last refrain,
I stand with pen in hand,
My plume, my last salute
To all the actors, all the makeup men.

Now let me take my bow,
No longer fearful of forgotten lines,
The frowning of a prompter,
The ever-present glare of lights.

The accolade, a mere echo from afar,
The curtains fall before my eyes,
Never to rise again—no rose today,
A daisy at my feet, my only prize.

The shuffling feet have ceased,
Torn tickets on the floor,
Attendants waiting at the door,
And silence echoes from the wings.

The Immigrant

Astride his suitcase,
His bronco on the quay,
Impatiently he waits,
The gate of Sesame to spring
And to be ferried
By capricious waves
Of a November stormy sea.

Wearily he looks
Upon the sea of dreams,
Down at the water's edge,
The lapping waves,
The blackened sea-encrusted piles,
The screeching gulls,
The shore-born surfers of the wind.

He is the father and the son
Of still-remembered dreams,
Of barren hills, the village stench,
The choking dust,
The wintry frost at night,
But there beyond the water's edge,
A misty sun of hopes had lit the sky,
As yet not fully born.

He wakens from his dreams.
It is a sound, a monody, a wail,
Soft like a song of old,
A summon to embark.
At last his ship had come
Upon the voyage of his dream,
The steamer and the sea,
To take him home.

The Lady on the Isle

"Keep ancient lands, your storied pomp!" cries she
With silent lips. "Give me your tired, your poor,
Your huddled masses yearning to breathe free,
The wretched refuse of your teeming shore.
Send these, the homeless, tempest-tossed to me,
I lift my lamp beside the golden door!"
—Emma Lazarus

Tranquil and serene, the autumn sea,
The foaming waves already spent,
The rolling of the ship had ceased,
And silently the ship plows through the morning tide.
The land of our dreams was near,
No longer a delusion, a mirage.

Wrapped in Aurora's mist,
There on the isle the lady stood,
Arm raised, and in her hand
A gilded torch, to light, to greet
The weary voyager, unwanted men—
"The huddled masses," "tempest tossed,"
The tired and the poor from far away.

By the salt-encrusted rail we stood,
Wounded dreamers of years gone by,
And gazing through the rising mist,
Looked at Bartholdi's mother's somber face,
Read Emma's invite to the shore ahead.
Some read the words, some wept, some smiled.

With license to transform,
I saw the lady once before.
She stood by other open gates,
No torch to greet "beside the golden door."
She stood before me, helmeted, arm raised,
A warrior's sword in hand,
Pale, horror-struck her gentle face.

And as I looked at her,
A prisoner's grateful eye,
I wondered why she came.
What kept her waiting, sword in hand?
And why she came so late
While millions perished,
The hapless victims of a tyrant's hate.

Unpublished Words

At ease the trembling hand,
The faithful pen had ceased to write.
Words born, then cradled on a page,
Become imprisoned thoughts.

Like wing-clipped birds of song
Confined are silent in their cage,
Begging the passersby to read,
Begging to be heard.

Even the mute man sings;
Only his ears can hear the silent chords.
The blind man sees, illumined by an inner light,
A light that none but he alone can see.

So let the words remain at rest
In prose or in poetic rhyme,
For words once formed
Become the obelisks of time.

The Stranger

I knew him once, a friend, a chum of mine.
His grin of youth had given way
To grimace, to a wrinkled brow,
His trembling hand, once master of a pen,
His songs, his words, a blur by now.

He stares, but to his curtained eye,
Milky the dawn, mist-veiled the sunset,
Longer the shadows at day's end—
The pendulum of time is nearly spent.

He was a chance witness
Of much ruin, carnage, floods,
Each ending in a rainbow promise,
While a new deluge followed
Before the last was gone.

A stranger now in a surging crowd,
Adrift he can no longer stem the tide.
With limping gait he shuffles on,
The past a witch's Sabbath,
The future a portentous end.

With pleading eye he shuffles on,
Then hesitates, the man without a name,
A name beyond recall,
A stranger now, a stranger to himself,
A stranger to us all.

The Eyes

Blessed be the eyes
That out of cozy darkness
First saw the light,
Then saw a mother's face.

Blessed be the eyes,
Unfailing servants of the heart,
That bid them to behold
The petal of a rose at dawn.

Eyes, windows of the self,
The wordless orators
Of a thousand idioms
When words began to fail.

Eyes that gaze within myself,
Sagacious judges on some sunless day,
Knowing to pardon, knowing to absolve
When wisdom and my judgment fail.

Thou Shall Not Kill

"Yummah, Yummah!" Fatima weeps.
"Oh, Allah Acbar!" Our God is great,
Tears streaming down her lacerated face.
"Mayn kind, mayn kind!" Rebecca wails.
"Adonai, eykhod!" Our God is one.
She beats her breasts.
"Rebyata, oy rebiata!" Nadyezhda screams.
"Oh Bozhe moy, oh Bozhe moy!"
"My God, my God!"
And with her fingers claws the frozen tundra soil.

It is their language of despair
For murder of a child,
A child, their flesh, the essence of their being—
Negates the miracle of birth.

And so they lament, so they weep,
Their voices meant to reach
The ears of Allah, Christos, Adonai,
Not men, but man-made Gods,
Gods who have fashioned men.

It is the Gods that lit in some men's breast
The need to torture and to kill,
Deaf to mother's tears,
It is their morbid thrill.

But there are men who weep with them
And walk and walk with signs aloft.
"Peace on Earth, thou shall not kill,"
Their signs proclaim.

While others, sword in hand
And vengeance in their plumes,
Cry, "War upon such men!"
In time they too will go,
And heeding God's design
With righteousness at heart,
They too will maim and kill.

The Sparrow

We were children, Ben and I,
The world our meadow
To frolic in and romp
The backyard pond our sea.

Ben grew to be a man,
Tall, unabashed, light-footed,
The world a pageant and he the peacock
With plumage fan in full array,
A dandy man, a popinjay.

One day the knell of time
Struck like a thief at night.
It struck the senses without
Reason, without rhyme,
In brutal dissonance.

With chin upon his chest,
Ben's speech, a rasping slur,
Bereft of plumage of the years,
His nest with ashes strewn,
A bird of prey, wing-clipped,
A wounded sparrow now.

It Spins

Spinning within its orbit of eternity,
The matins and vespers,
Only illusions made by man,
Invented just to count the time,
To count the cosmic span.

Hiding from the burning sun,
The lustrous sea, the earth,
The wrinkled lands,
The night, an invitation
To recall the day gone by.

Then one more half-turn of the globe,
And dawn dispels the burden of the dark.
A sultry night had given way
To mist-laden droplets on a petal of a rose,
Ushering a newborn, gentle day.

When hope is hope reborn,
Tap dancing and hand clapping,
Garden days in bloom,
The ever-thirsty hummingbirds
In duets with the bumblebees.

And so the earth does turn.
And so does our frame of mind,
The ebbing and the rising of the tide,
Our merriment and past recall
The thoughts of who we were
And who we are today.

The Gates of Hell

Upon the president's visit to Auschwitz
June 1, 2003

"Lasciate ogne speranze   voi ch'intrate queste parole di colore
oscuro. Vid'io scerite all sommo d'una porati …"
"All hope abandon ye who enter here. These words in
somber written upon the summit of a gate …"
—Dante Alighieri, "The Inferno"

Walk gently, for the dust and clay
Still groan with every step of yours
And asks, have you been blind?
Have you been deaf?
When children, naked, hair-shorn, begged,
"I promise to be good,
Just let me live, for just one little while,"
And with their parents hand in hand walked to their doom.

Look at the sky, unclouded now,
Azure, unblemished by the clouds
Of smoke, of burning flesh,
The messages to Gods above,
And to those righteous men below,
Of White House lawns, of Downing Street,
The Kremlin and rose gardens

Look, modern emperors and queens,
At the steely railroad tracks,
Placed there to haul away in cattle cars,
To jettison the detritus,
Believers in a God of long-gone days.
Do not avert your newfound Christian eyes.
Look now and pray.

In Search of Myself

How often have I searched
The road to tell me who I am?
And mystified by many signs,
I wondered where they led.

And then misled, that in the end
All roads led somewhere.
The safest one to take
Would be the road into myself.

Homeward bound, it led,
Weather-beaten, rock-strewn,
Sun-splashed, familiar footprints
Showing me the way.

I trudged along, foot-sore,
Parched and with tired leg,
The horizon of my aim
Receding with each step.

And when I got there by and by,
Tired and with halting breath,
The road came to an end.
"Stop here and gaze!"
A full-length mirror said.

The image convoluted, warped,
Bandy-legged, a grinning clown,
Clodhoppers on my feet,
A spooky apparition, stood I,
Half tearful and half smile.

And so I stood and realized
It simply wasn't worth the effort.
It simply wasn't worth the time.
The image wasn't I,
Or was it?

Imagination

I dreamed I was the king of kings,
A wealthy potentate,
My royal residence a treasure trove
Of things I gathered one by one
By means of amity, by means of wars.

A lifelong aggregate
Of precious gems,
Of sculpted handiwork,
The silks of distant lands,
My floors were gilded tiles.

Exquisite art adorned my walls
To fit my opulent abode.
Pure golden was my scepter and my crown,
My robe, silk-woven,
And at my side a ceremonial sword.

Soft silken were my cushions
To entice and to allure
An Eve, a Venus, an Aphrodite,
To quench my longing arms
If only for a single tryst.

Then startled by an avian song
I suddenly woke up to realize
No brocade cushion there.
My head is resting on the bark
Of my shade-giving tree.

My treasures though are there,
The ruby is my crimson summer rose,
Gold dust residing in my lily's heart,
The silken moss, a damsel's soft caress,
The ferns and spiderwebs my filigrees.

Sweet berries my provender here,
The blue jays and the mockingbirds,
One my court jester, the other one my bard,
Tall stand my hollyhocks and glads,
My ever-faithful royal guards.

My crown, a straw hat now,
The denim overalls, my royal gown,
The cutters, hoe, the wooden rake,
The workmen's leather gloves,
My scepter and the mace.

It is the realm of open gates,
No drawbridge and no moats,
No ramparts and no canons here,
The garden is my sovereignty,
And here I sway supreme.

To Rest, To Sleep

"To sleep: perchance to dream …"
—William Shakespeare, *Hamlet*

Rest at ease, the faithful pen,
Even the tallest elm at season's end
Must shed its leaves.
The mighty bear, the lion in his den,
Must hibernate to gather strength
To rule supreme again.

They say the spirit,
Like the most fertile soil,
Must be permitted to lie fallow,
To be fruitful once again.
The windblown seed
Embedded in its womb
Must find its heart and learn to throb.

The bard's most joyous song must end,
And so the writer's hand
Needs to desist, or else
His rhymes turn formless, shallow,
His thoughts a parched and arid land,
And the most nimble fingers
Must cease to pluck the harp.

Awakened by the wind,
The sleeping butterfly unfolds its wings,
The night to dream is gone,
And born again it heeds the call
And heads for home again.
The writer's pen, stirred from its sleep,
Begins to scribble in half-dream.

The Thirteenth Chime

The clock struck suddenly again,
The thirteenth beat, harsh,
Unlike the others, a deadly knell,
An alien chime, pain-racked,
Gripped by a crushing fear.

The limelight dimmed,
And suddenly a gloomy dusk
Eclipsed the shadows on my moonlit stage.
The wheels of time began to slow.
The gears of all my being ceased to mesh.

They slowed but didn't cease to turn,
And all the rivers ceased to flow.
The road ahead had reached its end.
"Nothing beyond," the road sign said,
And with my lips compressed,
Silently I begged, *Not yet, not yet.*

With a pain-constricted throat,
I was the beggar, begging for some alms,
For just another day,
A grant, an offering, a gift of stay,
But there was stillness
And forbidding.

A spark lit far away,
Soft whispers, fluttering of lips
Of other men, not mine,
Masked, lead-clad, aproned
With knitted brows,
All gazing at a glassy screen.

A man's face hidden by a mask,
A guiding catheter in hand,
I felt the ebbing of my pain
And stillness of the night
Gave rise to a soft tune of rippling waves.
The river flowed again.

He spoke, "Look, look, it beats
A normal rhythm. It's back again"—
A whisper with a solemn ring,
Tough to my empty ears. It was a shout;
I knew it all too well.
They spoke of life and death.

In doubt whose life was on the scale,
Light flooded once again the darkened stage.
The pain was gone, and I perceived
That life grew wings, my river flowed again,
And she stood there. The guardian beyond the screen
Was there to watch, to nurture, to sustain.

The Lover

I've seen you make love
Wherever you wished,
On an ice-covered pond
Or soft green moss.

On the sidewalk,
In the backyard, or in the middle of the street,
In the neighbor's flower bed,
None too discreet.

At sunrise or at dusk,
A sunlit sky or a full moon,
You lady-killer, Don Juan,
At midnight or high noon.

Be she brunette with ringlet hair,
Voluptuous, dainty-legged,
Or with the shape of a teddy bear,
You love them just the same.

And in your tryst you do not care,
Softly caressed, love-bitten in the neck,
As long as it is she
Who gives a heck.

You part without adieu,
With a lusty bark and waggling tail.
You pounce upon your Alpo dish,
You sexy hero of the day.

Professor Le Roach

As Professor Le Roach,
It is my duty to teach
As best as I know,
Without bias or slightest reproach,
The story of humans of eons ago.

A biped, he of brittle skin,
Sans wings, sans antennae, sans grace,
Abhorrent, hateful was his grin,
On his sordid humanoid face
As he sought our doom
With his foot and his broom.

Homo Sapiens, he called himself.
Homo what? with doubt do I say.
And as I look at the past,
I fervently hope, I fervently pray,
He's been gone forever,
Gone, vanished at last.

Look back at his Gods at hand.
One sat in the shade of a tree,
Another one armed with a magic wand,
A master of plagues and the parting sea,
A fisherman wrapped in a shroud,
A camel man and his angel with wings,
And at last the great mushroom cloud.

Gods full of vengeance,
The last one filling the sky,
Erasing the sun in its fiery path,
And in a flash like the flip of a wing of a fly,
Man's reign was finished,
Gone without saying as much as good-bye.

We're free now, three cheers and hooray,
Six-legged brethren with feathered antennae,
Walking with stealth in brown camouflage,
No need to hide any longer, no need to flee,
Beneath a cupboard or the creaking stair.

And so at dawn as you leave your den,
Raise your head and fold your wings.
Gaze with awe at the sky,
And with a murmur fervently pray,
For there resides our king of all kings,
The great cockroach with his fiery eye,
And tired at night our mother the moon
Takes her turn as she softly glides by.

I Know You

I know the throb of your heart,
The drumbeat echoes
Of so many words unspoken,
Words winged and words sublime,
Unspoken still at dawn,
Merely a hush at eventide,
But in the stillness of the night
Uttered with every sigh.

I know the sculpture of your thighs,
Unseen but mirrored in each step,
The soft-curved breasts
With every breath,
The ebbing and the falling tide,
The nodding of your head
In cadence with your thoughts,
In silent discourse with yourself.

And yet the many thoughts
You harbor in the safety
Of the source of life,
The fig leaf mystery,
Pandora's gifts of pain and hope—
These I shall never know,
So let it be, for you are woman
And I am only man.

The Gourmand

I am the nibbler of good food,
A guzzling, swilling bon vivant,
The finger-licking epicure
Of chicken à la king
And chicken cacciatore.

But best of all, I like the chicken
Strutting down the dusty road,
Worm picking, cackling,
The wing-spread chick,
The morning cockatoo.

The picker, dainty feeder,
With lusty eye I ogle
Fresh roasted ham,
Orange-glazed spareribs.

And yet how fondly I behold
My porcine, squealing friend,
Gazing at me with beady eye
In its malodorous and dingy sty.

With trembling hand I cut
The juicy T-bone steak,
Garlic-refined beef provençale,
Grilled, roasted, even stewed.

And yet in quest of tranquil moods
I like my beef upon the lea,
The tail-swishing kind,
Its plaintive sunrise moo.

The skewered cubes of lamb,
Grilled, marinated chops,
The cutlets and the stew
A glutton's ecstasy, a sheer delight.

And yet my eye prefers to feast
Upon the rolling hills,
The romping ewes and rams,
And listen to their baas.

Bel Canto

So much of our lives are songs,
Some our own, some borrowed,
Like mockingbirds, the mime,
Slavish in semblance and disguise.

A rocking cradle lullaby
To still a thirsty infant's cry,
A toddler's bandy-legged walk
And squeal of joy.

A young boy's lusty yell,
The rumpled hair,
The wings upon his restless feet,
The sky, the wind his heir.

The trumpet call to walk,
To march in step to be alike,
The head held high
In martial stride.

A dandy's whistle
In his evening prowl,
A wedding march,
A softly whispered vow.

And later on a dirge,
A sorrowful regret,
A friend once prospered
And died in pain.

I, for one, go on to sing my song,
A not too softly chiming bell.
Mine is a coda of the past,
Not yet a farewell.

The Listener

I've ceased to listen to the thunder
Of waves pounding, crashing
Over moss-covered boulders,
Lashed by sun-dried weeds,
Waves heaving, surging against
The rocky shores of yesterdays.

Now I only hear the mist-wrapped,
Moonlit whispers of a tranquil sea,
The rasping melody of sand,
Faint echoes of a conch,
The cries of a lonely albatross,
Skimming the cresting waves.

In my half dream of long ago,
Free of terror, free of fear,
Perceived by fading ears,
Lip-reading I can only hear
The snare-drum song
Of pebbles by the ebbing tide.

That Ole Man River

Quiet runs my river,
No longer winding, twisting,
Mountain streams
Peaceful now.

Unspent the foaming waves,
Tired and chilled,
Autumnal leaves adrift,
Reluctantly it flows
Upon the gathered silt.

In river-dream recall
Of chafing, rushing waves
Through gorges, canyons
Chilled by crumbling glaciers,
Then warmed by pelting rains.

Soft waters once,
Then bittersweet,
Once halted by a dam,
Then freed again
And joined by other streams.

Nearly home and spent,
It spreads its swanlike wings
To brace horizons tranquil sea,
To be reborn in its domain,
To dream again.

And like that ole man river,
He don't say nothin',
But must know somethin'.
He just keeps rollin'.
He just keeps rollin' along.

To Be Alive

While day by day and often
During sleepless nights,
We gaze with half-averted eyes.
Without much sorrow, without a tear,
We look upon the sallow skin,
Upon the somnolent, the sunken cheeks,
The swollen belly of a child.

The raging hate, the villages on fire,
The maimed, the crippled,
Charred remnant of a dwelling,
Bomb shredded, stained attire,
The ravaged and the raped,
Begging for mercy, asking for help.

So raise your chalice, doff your hat,
Sing praise to Dante's hell.
Drink up, drink up, my fellow man.
Drink up, be calm,
Your remedy, your balm,
While others lower caskets,
And in their idioms whisper, "Dust to dust,"
Into the earthen realm.

Must I Forget?

"There is no remembrance of former things;
Neither shall there be any remembrance of things
That are to come with those that shall come after."
—Ecclesiastes 1:11

At last the sun has set,
The night about to spawn,
Perhaps reluctant of another dawn.
The past is set to take its flight
On wings of evanescence.

Must I, the weary wanderer,
Forget the cradlesong,
The wind-born lilts of yesterday,
The mesmerizing pendulum,
Pacemaker to my daily life?

Must I forget a mother's lilt,
Cradling her newborn against her milk-ripe breasts,
The schoolboy's restless feet beneath the bench,
The sparrow on the windowsill
In duet with the teacher at the desk?

Or the first rays at dawn,
Mist-laden shafts of light,
Skipping over the rippling brook,
Two butterflies, two snowflakes
In their summer flight.

The hoofbeat sound,
The early morning milkman's cart
Over the wooden bridge,
The old man snapping whip,
His sleepy urging slang.

The throaty chanting of a frog
Concealed within a clump of reed,
And then another one, the caw
Of the black raven,
Of tear-stained days, of days of awe.

And then another song,
The blessing on a cup of wine,
The shattered glass, a blushing bride,
Soft whispers in the night,
The whimper of a hungry child.

Gaudeamus, as we rejoice,
Clad in a borrowed cap and gown,
A smile with head held high,
A necklace stethoscope,
A steady hand and well-trained eye.

Must I forget a grandchild's
Tinny song, the garlands from afar?
These are the sounds of my delights,
Beyond erase of time,
Etched and indelible these sights.

Delusions

Strutting upon a trembling soil,
The fire just beneath our feet,
We think we are the masters,
Full of confidence, full of conceit.

Without feathered wings we fly.
Without gills we swim, we dive,
Self-appointed rulers of the sea, the sky,
The larks at dawn, the bats at night.

But we are only butterflies of time,
A flash, the blinking of an eon's eye,
A speck,
A bit of dust in the cosmic sky.

We are the windblown kites,
Intoxicated by our might,
Adorned with hope
In our heedless flight.

Without ears attuned
To the shifting currents
Of all prevailing moral storms,
Wind-driven we remain afloat.

And yet we all are tethered
To a hand as yet unknown,
Unknowingly we drift, we err,
Into the coming bliss or blight.

And so pretending
We must sing,
Recite our mantras,
Inveterate dreamers
Of a promised land.

Of Doubt

Who set the clock
Of night and day,
A clock that never went astray?

Who swirled the electrons,
Then set them in their spin,
And multiplied their kin?

Who ruled that silver
Tarnishes in time,
But gold must always shine?

Who ruled that daffodils
Must wilt at summer's drought,
While other flowers sprout?

Who ruled that stones we trod upon
Or pass them by forever last,
But men must ail and all must die?

Who ruled that every spring
A rose is born according to some plan,
While other seeds will make a man?

Let Not the Children Die

Let not the howling dogs of hunger
Be an infant's cradlesong.
Let not the desert flies
Forever quench their thirst
In children's eyes.

Come, all you sons and daughters
Of the crescent scimitar,
The holy cross,
The lotus man,
The blue-white star.

Your tears alone,
Your songs of woe,
Your wringing hands
Will not abate the hunger
Of a single child.

No rubies, gilded diadems
Will seed the arid desert soil,
Will bring the rains,
Make ancient rivers flow
Through sandy desert lands.

The swollen bellies,
The outstretched hands
To Gods will not suffice,
Nor the soft whimper,
Nor the lament, nor the sigh.

No drumbeat, tenor, no cantata
Will ever feed a hungry child,
For it is white-robed man
With turban from another clan
That kills the seed
And kills the infant in its mother's arm.

My Seven Deadly Sins

While some were born to sainthood,
Their halos like a miner's lamp,
Casting light wherever they walk,
Flash-warning of each tempting snare,
Righteously they trod along
Their hallowed saintly paths.

I, for one, was born to sin,
And as I walk with crooked stealth,
No halo floats above my head,
Only a burglar's lamp
With hardly a flicker of light.

I hear the angels
Play their gilded harps,
Flapping their wings serenely,
I stand in silence,
Catlike sly in my disguise.

Bare-bottom, rubicund,
They pluck their little harps,
Falsetto-voiced sing their hosannas,
But I stomp my feet,
I kick my legs, I clap my hands,
My face an everlasting grin.

I laugh at them and thumb my nose.
Mine is a virtue that they lack
In poetry or prose.
I am the pleasure man,
The matchless paragon
Of all the seven deadly sins.

The Time Has Come

The time has come to be at ease,
The nameless voyager of yesterday,
Once rootless without home,
Foot-sore, the wanderer,
Stumbling along with tired sway
Along the dusty country roads,
The fugitive, the runaway.

The time has come to cease
To dream of wings,
Of ornate feathers in my hat,
Of gazing at the signposts,
Of promises betrayed,
Of once upon a time,
Of roads I strayed.

The time has come
To be at ease at last,
Inhale the fragrant scent
Of springtime trees abloom,
And dream along the shifting
Clouds of wishful thoughts,
And to forget the heartbreak days
Of things that should have been,
The days that now are naught.

Know Thyself

I am the fisherman, the angler,
Tireless seeker.
I am the quarry,
Short-lived, ephemeral,
My pen, the fishing rod,
My quest the evanescent lure
To find at last, to know
Of who I am.

The river, the pebbly shore,
And down below,
Beneath the rippling waves,
Swiftly and with stealth flit by.
My life,
In ever-changing flow,
Escapes my searching eye.

The sun had set,
Gilding the rippling waves.
My fishing net is empty now.
Exhausted is my pen.
My vision dimmed,
Long and illusive the shadows
Of who I think I am.

And so each day
I cast anew my line
Into the ever-changing stream,
For I was told
That I must find myself,
And so I fish.
I fish and wonder why.

The Ballad of the Missing Rib

One rib had vanished in my dream,
Gone, snatched from me,
Robbed, stolen without my consent,
Capriciously by an unknown hand,
A deed I couldn't understand.

With full resolve to get it back
By any means was my intent.
Down Eden Street I went,
The serpent basking in the sun
With a sly grin just shook his head.

The bearded scholar, staff in hand,
Ceased writing, lost in thought,
Then shrugged, and turning
To the tablets in his lap
Continued scribbling once again.

And so I walked and walked
Until I came upon a stream,
And in the shade a maiden sat,
A loaf of bread, a jug of wine,
A paintbrush in her hand.
Her name was Thou,
And so we sat to chat.

Sloe-eyed, crimson lips, and fair,
Lithesome and raven-black hair,
It set my heart aflutter.
I tasted of her wine and some,
And all I could utter was a stutter.

Beneath the silken canopy we stood.
Roses of Sharon, her face was veiled
From the cup of wine we took a sip
While the preacher spoke his last refrain:
"I now pronounce you Man and Rib,"
And I was whole again.

Join Me

I call upon you, those gently touched by age,
The slightly stooped and wrinkled brow.
Come lift your heads and sing again
Your long-forgotten songs.
Sing them, recite them with brush and pen,
And paint new colors to the dimming sky.
Add flavor into the mountain streams
And melodies to autumn winds.
Compel your pen to say the things
You only dared to dream.

Let Me Dream Awhile

My face against the windowpane,
I search with heavy-lidded eyes,
A beggar's longing hand
Asking for his alms
Of dreams that were withheld, denied.

Dawn comes at last, gray-flushed
Above the hilly crest.
It comes with an old man's tardy walk,
With a sigh of remorse for yet another day
That vanished, never to return.

With heavy-lidded eyes,
Still clamoring for sleep,
I gaze upon the mist-wrapped hills,
The scrub oaks bending low,
An empty raven's nest still clings
To a denuded branch, a dream.

Gone is the fragrance of lavender,
The pungent scent of eucalyptus,
The farewell attar of a wilted rose,
Adrift in the rustling wind.
It is the end of one more year.

And then a flash, a sudden glow,
A flicker of sunrise across the crest,
And awed I wish to greet the rising sun,
But song and rhyme does not suffice,
And so I greet the coming day
In grateful silence.

Let the Wounds Heal

Let silence fall upon the past,
Sever the shackles and the bonds,
The yoke, the heavy burden,
The twilight shadows cast.

Bid farewell to what
Unwilling eyes beheld.
Erase the echoes
Of the anguished cries.

Let heal the wounds of yesterdays,
The hidden sores,
Those camouflaged,
Concealed by smiles.

And while your eyes
Still search in vain
For comfort in the rippling waves,
In an elusive mountain stream.

Abandon fear,
The stream no longer tinged
By crimson waves,
Now crystal clear.

The clatter of the wheels
Upon the wooden bridge,
It is the milkman's horse
No longer stepping hobnailed heels.

The nettle weeds
Have lost their sting.
The dandelions' milky sap
Turned sweet again.

In Praise of Sound

I still can hear
The flutter of a hummingbird,
The chirping sparrow in its flight,
The springtime raindrop songs
Upon my roof at night.

I pray let not the silence
Of the spheres beyond,
The hush of everlasting nights,
Erase the cooing of a newborn babe,
The playful laughter of a child.

Let not the hush of sleep,
Eternal sleep bereft of sound,
Efface the avian plaintive melodies
And fervent whispers in the night

Let me still hear the vibrant
Resonance of cello strings,
The echoes of a far-off thunder,
The droning of a bumblebee,
The flutter of its wings.

Let me remain the man of songs,
With words, with pen,
Before the clock of time
Has run its course
Into eternal nights.

Ashes to Ashes

"Do not go gentle into that good night
... rage, rage against the dying of the light."

No, Dylan Thomas,
Go and rage.
I have no time to fume,
To vent my ire
To kick, to trash,
To set my soul on fire.

No, Dylan Thomas,
No, not me, I shall be busy
Watching autumn leaves
Fall to their wintry ground
In silence of the coming night
To where we all are bound.

No, Dylan Thomas,
To rage, to rant? you said.
I shall be way too busy
To gather all the gifts of life
Received with our neonatal cry
First smile, first frown,
First laughter, and first tear.

I shall be too busy to recall
In letters bold,
In letters faint or small,
Some best forgotten,
Some to be sung in rhythm and rhyme,
Some in a tenor grosso,
Some in a silent hum.

And having wished adieu
To stormy days of years gone by,
I shall gift wrap the rainbow,
The one to never flood again,
Only a chunk of it, a thimbleful,
Only a bit of the setting sun
Before it dips below the crest,
A fragment of an ogling moon,
A star, and all the rest.

In my falsetto voice
That none but I can hear,
I shall declaim
God bless an eagle's wing,
A fluttering stripe
Of red and blue and white,
A greeting lady by the sea,
Holding a torch,
A greeting issued just for me.

And when at last I close my eyes,
Let ashes to ashes, in ashes' idiom,
Whisper, let him be the man he was,
Dull at times or bright,
And let no kaddish be my elegy—
Only the giggle of a little child.

The Dreamer

I dreamed I was the king of kings,
A wealthy potentate,
My royal residence a treasure trove
Of things I gathered one by one
By means of amity, by means of wars.

A lifelong aggregate
Of precious gems,
Of sculpted handiwork,
The silks of distant lands,
My floors were gilded tiles.

Exquisite art adorned my walls
To fit my opulent abode.
Pure golden was my scepter and my crown,
My robe, silk-woven,
And at my side a ceremonial sword.

Soft silken were my cushions
To entice and to allure
An Eve, a Venus, an Aphrodite,
To quench my longing arms
If only for a single tryst.

Then startled by an avian song
I suddenly woke up to realize
No brocade cushion there;
My head is resting on the bark
Of my shade-giving tree.

My treasures though are there,
The ruby is my crimson summer rose,
Gold dust residing in my lily's heart
The silken moss, a damsel's soft caress,
The ferns and spiderwebs my filigrees.

Sweet berries my provender here,
The blue jays and the mockingbirds—
One my court jester, the other one my bard—
Tall stand my hollyhocks and glads,
My ever-faithful royal guards.

My crown, a straw hat now,
The denim overalls, my royal gown,
The cutters, hoe, the wooden rake,
The workmen's leather gloves,
My scepter and the mace.

It is the realm of open gates,
No drawbridge and no moats,
No ramparts and no canons here,
The garden is my sovereignty,
And here I sway supreme.

My blissful reverie
Still clinging to my tired eyes,
And as I look with awe,
I wonder, was it all a dream,
Or am I dreaming now?

The Fiddler on the Roof

Old man, you bard of yesterday,
Each day from sunrise until dusk
You sat there on the roof,
Bestowing melodies,
The sustenance of those of want,
To soothe all those in sorrow,
To give them hope
When hope became extant.

You played your tunes
While in the narrow village lanes.
The children sang
And barefoot kicked the dust,
The cackling chicken, lowing cows,
A rural symphony a ballad
As rich or as poor as life bestows.

And you looked down,
And crinkly-eyed you smiled,
The melodies a rosin to you bow,
To softly glide upon
The strings in rhythm and rhyme.

It didn't last forever, though,
For then one day
You gazed at those below
And saw the empty dusty roads.
The listeners down below were gone,
And suddenly you ceased to play.

It was a day
Of sorrow and of gloom,
The fiddle still beneath your chin,
The nimble bow devoid of strings,
And flail your arm
And trembling hand,
Tears flowing down your beard.

Gone were the lilting songs,
The once dulcet melodies,
Replaced by pealing bells,
By shouts of discord.
Run, run, my children.
Run, run, and hide
Before it is too late.

He disappeared, the fiddle man,
His fiddle now a dream,
Or could it have been
A fantasy, the melody
That wafted through the air,
A melody of sadness, joy,
Without a trace forever gone?

Self-Portrait

Dim the memory
Of that first blush of being,
The halting steps,
The fledgling years
Of slingshot, bow and arrow,
Swashbuckling days
Of make-believe and daring.

How wistfully I grope
For the once nimble wings
That kept me aloft.

Dream wings they were,
Now shorn,
Clipped one by one
By the tempests of time,
Bent, stoop-shouldered now,
Unsteady my walk,
Lines drawn upon my brow.

A blur, my penmanship,
I write, I hesitate, I start anew
In search of meaning,
Of relevance of words,
My syntax, sentences askew.

But pen in hand
In days of doubt
Of who I am,
Before I become stranger
To myself,
I look upon my child
And I am blessed,
A ray of morning light
Upon his smiling face,
And wonder why the quest.

Delusion

Strutting upon the trembling soil,
The fire just beneath our feet,
We are the self-deluded fumblers,
Full of confidence, full of conceit.

Without feathered wings we fly.
Without gills or fins we swim, we dive.
We are the rulers of the sea, the sky,
The larks at dawn, the bats at night.

We are the butterflies of time,
The blinking of an eon's eye,
An evanescent speck, a mote,
The dust in cosmic mist.

The windblown kites, we are
Intoxicated by our heights,
Adorned with hopes
In our heedless flights.

With our ears tuned into
Whimsies of all the currents, we gloat,
Of all prevailing storms,
Wind-driven we remain afloat.

Yet tethered we all are
To a hand as yet unknown,
And so we blunder
Into tomorrow's still unknown.

And so pretending
To be one and all,
Self-deluded do we sing
Te Deum and hosannas,
And to our hopes we cling.